The Twenty People You Meet In Hell

10-25-08

MaryAnn —

No, you're <u>not</u> in this book. God's blessings to you and Joe!

Judi Lindsey

Also by J. Taylor Ludwig

It Was Never About Books: Conversations Between A Teen And Her Pastor

The Twenty People You Meet In Hell

Judi Ludwig

iUniverse, Inc.
New York Lincoln Shanghai

The Twenty People You Meet In Hell

Copyright © 2008 by Judi Ludwig

All rights reserved. No part of this book may be used or reproduced by any means, graphic, electronic, or mechanical, including photocopying, recording, taping or by any information storage retrieval system without the written permission of the publisher except in the case of brief quotations embodied in critical articles and reviews.

iUniverse books may be ordered through booksellers or by contacting:

iUniverse
2021 Pine Lake Road, Suite 100
Lincoln, NE 68512
www.iuniverse.com
1-800-Authors (1-800-288-4677)

Because of the dynamic nature of the Internet, any Web addresses or links contained in this book may have changed since publication and may no longer be valid.

The views expressed in this work are solely those of the author and do not necessarily reflect the views of the publisher, and the publisher hereby disclaims any responsibility for them.

Unless otherwise noted, all Scriptures quoted are taken from *God's Word*® Translation. Copyright ©1995 by God's Word to the Nations Bible Society. Used by permission of Green Key. All rights reserved.

ISBN: 978-0-595-45424-2 (pbk)
ISBN: 978-0-595-89737-7 (ebk)

Printed in the United States of America

Acknowledgments

Two very dear friends helped immensely with this book. Without their help, it would probably still be gathering dust on the drafting table. I regret that both wish to remain anonymous. God knows who they are, and I pray that he will bless both of them abundantly for their contributions.

Thank you to my best friend and confidant, a retired Lutheran pastor in Wisconsin, who is schooled in languages and who helped me to understand the original Greek of the New Testament. He spent the entire summer of 2007 pouring over the manuscript and clarifying those areas that may have been cloudy or would have caused confusion to many readers. His contributions are the heart and the soul of this work and help to tie everything together. He is truly a fisher of men.

Thank you to my long–time friend in St. Louis for spending many hours reading and editing the first draft of the manuscript. Her advice to pray and let the Holy Spirit guide the writing of the book was exactly what the manuscript called for.

Thanks to my husband Rick for his encouragement and support and for entertaining the kids while I wrote.

Thanks to Sawyer and Paxie for their patience and understanding during those times when Mommy felt led to write instead of play.

Thank you to my friend, Carl Ramsey, for sharing his computer expertise during the formatting stage of publication. He added a "dash" of professionalism to the layout.

All praise and thanksgiving to God the Father of Jesus for giving me the idea for this book and for guiding it through to completion. May everyone who reads it be blessed. May God reach those who are lost and lead them to true repentance and a relationship with Jesus.

"I'll be looking down on you ... or I might be looking up."

—Bernard "Bernie" Heitmann, jokingly, shortly before his death from cancer in November 1998.

But the cowardly, and untrustworthy, and the ritually unclean, the murderers, the male and female prostitutes, and the makers of poisons, and the idolatrous, and all who are people of the lie, they have earned their place in the lake that burns with fire and sulfur. This is the second death! (Rev. 21:8 RPD)

Introduction

Do you believe you're a Christian? Do you believe you're going to heaven when you die? Jesus came to restore the kingdom of heaven on the earth, which was lost when Adam and Eve sinned. With his death on the cross, Jesus opened the gates of heaven to those who believe in him as the only atonement for sin and confess him as Lord of their life—that is, they are born again from above. The born-again believer has made the Great Exchange, meaning he has exchanged his natural life and sin for Christ's life in him. The Holy Spirit enables the new believer to become spiritually alive in Christ so that he or she is no longer dead in trespasses and sins. (Eph. 2:1)

Plenty of books have been written about heaven and what Christians can expect to find when they get there. This isn't one of them. Most people will never see heaven because, "Many are invited but few of those are chosen to stay." (Matt. 22:14, Matt.7:13)

This book is about those who have not made the Great Exchange, regardless of what they *say* they believe or whether or not they go to church. It's about those who have relied on their own "goodness" and have decided to run their own lives, rejecting Jesus as Lord and Ruler of their lives.

There are four words in the original languages of scripture that are usually translated "hell." In the Old Testament of the King James Version, the Hebrew word *Sheol* is the unseen place, the place of the dead to this world but still having an existence. Saul used the witch of Endor to call Samuel up from his resting or sleeping place—from *Sheol*.

In the New Testament, the words in the original that have been translated as *hell* are *hades*, *Gehenna*, and *Tartarus*. Hades was also a Greek god as well as the underworld and realm of the dead. Gehenna was the always burning garbage dump in the Valley of Hinnom on the southwest side of Jerusalem. The ever burning fire became synonymous with hell.

Tartarus was thought of as a place below Hades where the vile sinners in heaven and earth made atonement or expiation for their sins. It is only used once in 2 Peter 2:4.

What happens as we die? When is a person able to be pronounced dead? There are all sorts of theories. In fact, some people claim that the soul remains near the body for three days after death. There's nothing in the Bible to back up this theory, so how anyone could prove that I'm not sure. I suppose it has to do with no clear definition of death in the Bible.

There is only one reference to a séance in the Old Testament. Samuel calls upon the witch of Endor to bring him back from his rest in Sheol. (1 Sam. 28:7) We don't know how long Samuel stuck around after dying, if at all. The Bible certainly knows nothing about the soul remaining. In Ecc. 12:7 the Word simply says that at death the earthly remains go to the ground from which it was taken, and the spirit returns to God.

To dispute the unsubstantiated theory that the soul remains in the body for three days after death, all we need to do is review what Jesus said to one of the thieves who was being crucified next to him. When the thief asked Jesus to remember him when he enters his kingdom, Jesus replies: "I can guarantee this truth: Today you will be with me in paradise." Jesus doesn't say that in three days the thief will join him in paradise, but today, the day of death. This statement leaves no room for debate about when the spirit leaves the body. It leaves at the moment of death.

Paul leaves no room for the soul remaining on earth when he describes what happens when we die in 2 Cor. 5:1–10. He concludes that section with these words: "All of us must appear in front of Christ's judgment seat. Then all people will receive what they deserve for the good or evil they have done while living in their bodies."

Paul is actually saying that everyone who dies goes to heaven. That's where Christ's judgment seat is. The tragedy is that not everyone will stay in heaven, and that's what makes hell so horrid. You've seen heaven and know of its joys and that God indeed *is*. You are sent to hell for any number of the reasons outlined in this book.

The good news for born-again Christians is that, even though they must appear before Christ's judgment seat, they will not be judged. They have already been made holy and righteous through Jesus' death on the cross and have been forgiven for all their sins. Unbelievers, however, will have to give an accounting and be judged of their sins by Jesus on judgment day.

> The Father doesn't judge anyone. He has entrusted judgment entirely to the Son so that everyone will honor the Son as they honor the Father. Whoever doesn't honor the Son doesn't honor the Father who sent him. I can guarantee this truth: Those who listen to what I say and believe in the one who sent me will have eternal life. I can guarantee this truth: A time is coming (and is now here) when the dead will hear his voice, and they will come out of their tombs.

> Those who have done good will come back to life and live. But those who have done evil will come back to life and be judged. I can't do anything on my own. As I listen to the Father, I make my judgments. My judgments are right because I don't try to do what I want but what the one who sent me wants. (John 5:22–30)

Hell is the physical place God prepared for the devil and the demon spirits who serve the devil. Other books have provided physical descriptions of hell in greater detail and have reported the torture, pain, isolation, and desperation of hell's occupants. The question I asked myself when researching this book was, "Who is in hell, and why are they there?"

The residents of hell are obviously there because of wrong or sinful choices they made while on earth. What were those choices? How can we avoid falling prey to the same damning sins? Who are those sinners whose sins weren't covered by Jesus' death on the cross and why?

The Bible clearly names those in hell—the liars, drunkards, sexually immoral, and others—whose names will not be found in the Lamb's Book of Life (a requirement for entering heaven). According to the Bible, a lot of people, including many who call themselves Christians, will claim hell as their eternal destination. The validity of the Bible won't be questioned. I assume if you've decided to read *The Twenty People You Meet in Hell*, you already know hell is a very real place, and you understand that every single word in the Bible has been breathed by God.

A family member said to me, "The God I know is a loving and forgiving God. I don't believe he would send anyone to a place like hell." Yes, God is a loving and forgiving God.

> He is patient for your sake. He doesn't want to destroy anyone but wants all people to have an opportunity to turn to him and change the way they think and act. (2 Pet. 3:9)

But God is also a just and righteous God. If there is no punishment for sin, where is justice? If sin can be tolerated by God, then how is God righteous and holy?

At every funeral I've attended, the minister has announced at some point that the deceased is now in heaven. Mourners discuss with each other how the person is out of pain, free of debt, and has no more worries because he or she is now with God. If you attend enough funerals and listen to the ministers, relatives, and friends discussing their dearly departed, you'll begin to wonder if anyone is really going to hell. Well, maybe some people will go to hell, but probably not anyone close to you, you think. The truth, whether you want to believe it or not, is that everyone most likely knows at least one person who took the wrong path and is spending eternity in hell.

I have known several people whom I assume didn't go to heaven. One who really stands out in my mind is *Jack, who died about ten years ago. I met Jack through my friend *Bess, with whom he was having an adulterous affair. Jack was raised Lutheran and believed in Jesus as the Son of God, but he lived his life as if he didn't know Jesus. He was in the bar every night, not just drinking, but getting drunk. His affair with Bess was the reason he spent so much time at the bar—to be with the object of his lust.

Jack died unexpectedly of a heart attack two months after his sixtieth birthday. He had gone to the hospital Emergency Room, complaining of chest pains, and was admitted. When visiting hours had ended and his wife had left to go home, Jack called and chatted with his mistress for awhile. Six hours later he was dead.

God gave Jack a wake–up call that night with symptoms of a heart attack. Jack had a small window of opportunity to consider his eternal destination, to repent of his sins, and to make a commitment to truly follow Christ. He may have done that after talking with Bess, and, if so, I'll be overjoyed to be reunited with him in heaven. If he didn't cry out to God that night, there's a very good chance he's in hell right now with the many other people who have rejected Jesus as Lord of their lives.

My biggest regret is that I didn't speak with Jack about Jesus or warn him about hell while he was living a life separated from God. The opportunity is lost forever. Why so many people don't take Jesus' word on this subject seriously, we'll never know here on earth. Jesus said: "Why do you call me Lord but don't do what I tell you?" (Luke 6:46)

Those who don't reject their sinful behaviors, accept Jesus' atoning death on the cross for them, and make Jesus Lord of their lives—living according to the Spirit instead of the flesh—have rejected God's plan for canceling their guilt. Those who insist on living their own way instead of God's way—that is, they have not allowed the Holy Spirit to work the Great Exchange—will not enter the kingdom of God.

> The real light, which shines on everyone, was coming into the world. He was in the world, and the world came into existence through him. He went to his own people, and his own people didn't recognize him. However, he gave the right to become God's children to everyone who believed in him. These are people who haven't been born in a physical way—from a human impulse or

> from a husband's desire to have a child. Their birth was from God. The Word became human and lived among us. We saw his glory. It was the glory that the Father shares with his only Son, a glory full of kindness and truth. (John 1:9–14)

Dear reader, it is not my intention to hurt or offend you, but I would rather do that than see you go to hell. You have the power and the choice to reject the Holy Spirit's call and, by doing so, choose hell as your everlasting destination. However, you *can* inherit the kingdom of heaven. God knows sinners can't change from sinful to sanctified living or clean themselves up without help. Through Jesus, God offers freedom from both the penalty *and* the bondage of sin.

> Praise the God and Father of our Lord Jesus Christ! God has given us a new birth because of his great mercy. We have been born into a new life that has a confidence which is alive because Jesus Christ has come back to life. We have been born into a new life which has an inheritance that can't be destroyed or corrupted and can't fade away. That inheritance is kept in heaven for you, since you are guarded by God's power through faith for a salvation that is ready to be revealed at the end of time. (1 Pet. 1:3–5)

Those who hold a universalism view—the notion that everyone goes to heaven when they die with the possible exception of a few rotten eggs—might think this book is judgmental. They are absolutely correct; it is judgmental. However, God is the judge. I am simply the messenger. The profile of every sinner mentioned in this book who faces eternal destruction comes straight from the Bible.

The inclusion and description of various sins throughout the book is necessary to give you an idea of what God is talking about when he refers to certain sins as being damnable. The names of those who have sinned have been changed. Are all these people destined for hell when they die? Not necessarily. They simply meet the biblical paradigm of sinners God says won't inherit the kingdom of heaven because of the condition of their hearts. Any or all of them can heed the Spirit's call, turn to the Lord, and have their hearts changed. It is from the changed heart that righteous behavior comes. It is the heart changed by God's grace that is received in heaven. Learn why there is so great a need to change and how to bring that change about.

You may ask: What are the author's qualifications to write this book? God could have chosen a theologian with advanced degrees to present this information, but he chose me. Why me? Because I was once the chief of sinners and one of the people you would meet in hell, having been in bondage to many of the sins discussed in this book. I know the way to get off the road to hell and on the path to redemption and forgiveness, and I would like to share that knowledge with you. Since no sin is worse than any other sin, the people you will meet in hell are presented in alphabetical order. Discussion questions for each chapter are included in the back of the book.

You are about to read the profiles of some of the people in hell. If they resemble you or someone you know in any way, please know that going to hell is a choice—one we make, not God. After reading this book, I hope you'll choose heaven.

Some names have been changed for spiritual protection.

1

The Adulterers

Why should you, my son, be intoxicated with an adulterous woman and fondle a loose woman's breast? Each person's ways are clearly seen by the Lord, and he surveys all his actions. A wicked person will be trapped by his own wrongs, and he will be caught in the ropes of his own sin. He will die for lack of discipline and stumble around because of his great stupidity. (Prov. 5:20–23)

*Kent was unfaithful to *Betty while they were still engaged, so it came as no surprise when he began an adulterous relationship with another woman shortly after he married Betty. The affair ended a few years later when the mistress tired of waiting for him to obtain a divorce. It didn't take Kent long to begin another affair and then another and another. At one point, he had an affair on one of his affairs and was being unfaithful to two women to whom he had made promises. He is now sixty-five, is still married to Betty, and is involved in an affair which began about six years ago.

Kent isn't alone in his philandering. Read some of the headlines on the covers of women's magazines during any given week, and you'll find many couples who are dealing with adultery. Some headlines read, What You Should Do When Your Spouse Cheats, How to Win Your Man Back from the Other Woman, Is Your Husband Cheating on You? Take This Quiz and Find Out, How to Cheat without Getting Caught. The articles are endless.

The adultery epidemic

Adultery is one of those sins in American culture that is so widespread it has been accepted as an "okay" sin. So many people engage in this sin we're tempted to change God's rules and not call it a sin. There are those who think if we refuse to accept adultery, then we're cutting too many people off the heaven list. If everyone is doing it, then we can't really call it a sin anymore, right?

Wrong! When we're looking at our two eternal choices of heaven or hell, it doesn't matter what society says; it matters what God says. God says adultery is a sin that is punishable by eternal damnation in hell if you do not repent of it and stop any adulterous conduct. True repentance means to change your mind about and turn away from the behavior, seeking God's forgiveness and desiring not to sin again.

Sex is part of God's design for a married couple to love each other and to come into greater intimacy with each other, as well as to procreate. God's Word tells us that when we have sexual intercourse, we become one with the other person. God designed that oneness to bring us peace and joy in an emotional environment of love and security. He wants us to be faithful as he is faithful. He designed marriage to be a model of his faithfulness to the world and to be a taste of the love, peace, joy, and intimacy of heaven. He is able to heal *any* marriage and restore it to a joyful experience. That's why he hates divorce so much. Divorce is a rejection of God's will for our living on this earth.

Many who have been married and divorced claim marriage is just a piece of paper, a certificate. God, however, says marriage is ordained to be a lifelong covenant which must be honored or there will be a tremendous penalty to pay.

> Those who commit adultery will not inherit the kingdom of God. (1 Cor. 6:10)

Let's not single out either gender when discussing this sin. It takes two people to commit adultery. Not all men who are cheating on their spouses are having affairs with single women. Married women are also committing adultery in alarming numbers.

For centuries adultery was considered a sin that was detestable to both God and men. Many now consider adultery an acceptable, even inevitable, problem of marriage, right along with financial problems, child–rearing problems, and the like. God doesn't see it that way.

> Marriage is honorable in every way, so husbands and wives should be faithful to each other. God will judge those who commit sexual sins, especially those who commit adultery. (Heb.13:4)

God says, as long as you are married, he expects you to have sexual intercourse unless one of the partners becomes unable to do so. This intimate emotional and physical relationship belongs only to marriage until death ends the marriage union. If you divorce and remarry for any reason other than that your spouse has been sexually unfaithful, then you are guilty of adultery with your new spouse.

> For example, a married woman is bound by law to her husband as long as he is alive. But if her husband dies, that marriage law is no longer in effect for her. So if she marries another man while her husband is still alive, she will be called an adulterer. But if her husband dies, she is free from this law, so she is not committing adultery if she marries another man. (Rom.7:2–3)

If you decide to proceed with divorce and remarriage, despite the fact that your former spouse was faithful, the person you marry is committing adultery as well as the spouse you divorced, if he or she remarries, along with their new spouse. One person's decision to commit adultery draws several people into adultery.

> Jesus said, I can guarantee that whoever divorces his wife for any reason other than her unfaithfulness is committing adultery if he marries another woman. (Matt.19:9)

If you have divorced your spouse for reasons other than unfaithfulness, what should you do now? Well, the last thing you want to do is to beat up on yourself and get yourself into covenant bondage. I know of two women who, since becoming born-again Christians, have decided God wants them to get back together with the spouses they divorced. One has been waiting for nine years and the other for eighteen years for something that is not likely to happen. If by some stroke of luck it does happen, it's not because God had his hand in it.

Both women, because they had made marriage covenants, believe they need to remarry their former spouses. The problem is that both of their former spouses are already married to other women, and one has already started a family. Does God want to break up these families and send the men back to their former spouses? Of course not! God doesn't want more hurt and pain and destruction, which is what divorce always breeds. Since it is the words spoken that make the covenant, these husbands already have broken their first covenant and entered into a covenant with their present spouses. This is the covenant that should be honored.

As for the women, they insist that it takes both partners to a covenant to break it—that it can't just be broken by *one* partner—and since they have not had sexual relations with anyone else since their divorces, then the marriage covenant is still intact. They want their men back—despite the fact that they have remarried other women! Unfortunately, they did break their marriage covenants upon signing their divorce papers, where they retracted the words they had spoken in their marriage covenant vows. They and their spouses, in essence, took the words back, thereby breaking their marriage covenant and forming a divorce covenant. Jesus said, "Let your yeses mean yes and your no's mean no." (Matt. 5:37) When these women signed their names to their divorce papers, they said no to their marriage covenants and yes to their new divorce covenants.

Jesus came to set the captives free. These women have not embraced the freedom Jesus won for them on the cross and allowed themselves to be free. Since their former spouses are already remarried, everyone involved can and should repent of the sins of divorce and adultery and move on to discover God's purpose for their lives now. Jesus has already forgiven these women for obtaining divorces and breaking their marriage covenants; now all they have to do is accept that forgiveness and forgive themselves. Satan will do everything within his power to keep them in bondage to marriages that don't exist.

An act of hate

Adultery is a very serious sin, but those who commit this sin choose not to see it that way. They will think of any reason they can to justify continuing in their adultery, even saying that God wouldn't send someone to hell for an act of love. Adultery is *not* an act of love, regardless of your fondness for the person with whom you are committing this sin. Adultery is an act of hate! It is an act of hate against your spouse and rebellion against God.

God has said he will forgive you if you are sorry for and reject your adulterous life and accept his Son Jesus as your Lord and Savior. Allow Jesus to be the captain of your ship. He wants to steer you away from dangerous reefs of sinful destruction by working in your heart through the power of the Holy Spirit.

> God is faithful and reliable. If we confess our sins, he forgives them and cleanses us from everything we've done wrong. If we say, "We have never sinned," we turn God into a liar and his Word is not in us. (1 John 1:9–10)

Temptation and the opportunity to commit adultery are always going to be there, but when the Great Exchange—exchanging your life for Christ's—has taken place, there is great power against that temptation because you now have the desire in your heart to love your spouse and to please God. Christ is at the center of the marriage, and the desire to please him is first priority at all times. Filled with God's love, each spouse seeks to please the other rather than please himself or herself. Small dissatisfactions with the spouse, marriage, or circumstances are immediately taken to the Lord in prayer before they become big problems and open the door to sexual and emotional temptation. The Holy Spirit is well able to keep spouses pure and loving toward each other, providing the power to resist temptation.

The sin of adultery can easily escalate into additional and sometimes deadly sins, as is evident in the following: A Lutheran minister from Kansas began having an affair with his secretary. Both were married, and each had several children. They approached a friend and asked him to murder their spouses. The friend suggested they divorce instead. Greed set in, and the two lovers decided it would be best to at least murder the secretary's spouse, who had taken out a $270,000 life insurance policy on himself a year before. The adulterous affair resulted in the murder of both of their spouses, and the two have been sentenced to life in prison. What had started as lust had led to adultery, then to greed, and finally to murder.[1]

Adultery is not always a premeditated sin. For many, adultery happens by "accident." A man runs into a woman he knew in high school. With their spouses' knowledge, they meet for lunch and discover they're both having some difficulties in their marriages. At this point, if either is a Christian, that person should say, "It was nice to see you and talk with you again after so many years, but I don't think we should continue to meet. Since we both have troubled marriages in need of healing, nothing good could come from us seeing each other again without our spouses present."

If they continue to meet, the chances of adultery not happening are very slim. Anytime members of the opposite sex are alone together for extended periods of time, the devil is going to tempt them with thoughts of adultery. The only way to avoid falling prey to this sin "accidentally" is never to put yourself in a situation where adultery could occur. Don't meet with a member of the opposite sex for any reason without your spouse present, regardless of how good a "friend" the person is or how confident you are you won't be tempted. It was for a very good reason that St. Paul was inspired to write: "Abstain from all appearance of evil." (1 Thess. 5:22 KJV)

Jesus said in the Sermon on the Mount, "But I can guarantee that whoever looks at a woman and desires her has already committed adultery in his heart." (Matt. 5:28) Temptations can't be helped. The devil, the world, and our own sinful flesh see to it that many temptations to break God's commandments will come our way. However, the sinful thought occurs when you make that temptation your own by either continuing to contemplate it or by deceiving yourself into thinking how great it would be to do it.

In domestic murder cases, adultery is cited as the number one reason why husbands murder their wives. In Iran and many other Arab countries, women who commit adultery are stoned to death.[2] Although Jesus hates adultery, he told those who were about to stone a woman to death for the sin, "The person who is sinless should be the first to throw a stone at her." (John 8:7) Adultery is a forgivable sin, and those who have committed this sin need only ask God's forgiveness, accept that they're forgiven, and give their hearts to the Lord, who will help them to grow in love and to remain faithful to their spouses in the future.

Premarital sex

If either or both of the participants in a sexual relationship do not consider their act of mating to be their marriage, it is not part of God's good plan for happiness and family life for this life. It doesn't matter if both partners are single. If one or both partners are married, they have committed the sin of adultery. If neither is married and they're having sex, they may be guilty of sexual immorality, prostitution, or sex for the mere pleasure of the moment.

The word most often used in the Bible for premarital sex is translated "fornication." It comes from the root word *porno–*, which means to purchase or to pay for an object or service. In regards to sex, *porno* means to engage in sex for some kind of consideration. Rewarding your date with sex for a nice evening and dinner on the town would be an example of *porno*/fornication. Any time sex is treated as a commodity, a reward, or a reciprocity, it is biblically *porneia*/prostitution. This type of sexual behavior indicates a heart that is far from God's character of love and faithfulness, thus making it a damning sin. For some reason, people have a hard time calling sex sin when it is between two consenting adults, but that's what God calls it when the two consenting adults do not consider their act of mating to be the formation of the new family unit.

A young woman said to me, "I don't know anyone who believes premarital sex is wrong anymore except you. You're just old–fashioned. If God is going to send everyone to hell who has sex before they're married, there won't be anyone in heaven."

> Therefore, many are invited, but few of those are chosen to stay. (Matt. 22:14)

This young woman should know that there are different standards of conduct for people who know what God says and for those who don't. A person who actually believes in Jesus—has received him as Lord, as well as Savior, and has made the Great Exchange—will follow the Spirit, not the desires of the flesh.

Sex outside of marriage has been considered a sin since the beginning of time, but now, all of a sudden, it's not a sin anymore? What changed? Certainly not God's Word. God tells us a marriage covenant, the formal public consent, is to be established before sexual relations take place. The word used in the New Testament for covenant is *dia–theke*. St. Paul uses this word in Gal. 3:15 to mean the inviolable last will and testament. Thus covenant means to make a permanent, binding agreement. Most often the covenant is a promise made by God to some person or group to establish God's faithfulness. In Genesis 9:8–16 God placed the rainbow in the heavens as a sign of his covenant that there would never again be a worldwide flood. God gave his commandments to Israel on Mount Sinai and promised the Israelites many blessings if they were faithful in obeying and keeping his commandments because then the curse of sin would be broken.

This covenant of mutual consent freely given is to be established before a couple engages in sex. When a couple has sex before marriage, they enter into a spiritual union and form soul ties with someone who is not their covenant partner. If they then move from partner to partner, they carry these soul ties into their other relationships. Instead of two joining to become one in marriage covenant, several souls are joining with several, destroying the framework of intimacy and faithfulness God intended. Couples who have engaged in premarital sex should repent of having had sex prior to marriage so that they can experience the intimacy that comes only from a single soul joining with a single soul.

Statistics show that if sex is casual outside of marriage, then it will be casual inside it as well. The devil has many lies he throws at us to try to convince us premarital sex is not a sin. Some of Satan's lies are that premarital sex creates intimacy, that sex early in a relationship will help you get to know the other person better so you'll become better sex partners later, that casual sex without long–term commitment is fun and freeing, that if you don't have casual sex, you must be repressed or prudish, and that God doesn't expect us to remain sexually pure in the twenty–first century. The truth is that promiscuous sex has been purported to cause dissatisfaction with a present marriage, unhappiness with the level of sexual intimacy in marriage, and low self–esteem, among other things.[3]

So is premarital sex wrong in every situation? Not necessarily. If a couple engaging in premarital sex considers their sex act to be mating and the formation of a new family unit, they have not sinned. For example, if an engaged couple has sexual intercourse before they're married, they haven't committed a damnable sin because, with plans to marry, they most likely consider the sex part of their mating. They have formed a covenant even though they haven't participated in the formal public ceremony yet. In determining if someone is in rebellion to his commandment not to commit adultery or *any* of his commands, God looks at hearts.

What about couples who are living together with no plans to marry? If an unmarried couple is living together, then one of them doesn't want to make a commitment. Sometimes both partners don't wish to commit. So couples who live together instead of marrying are basically saying, "This is just a temporary arrangement. I'm not in this relationship for better or worse, richer or poorer, in sickness or in health. I'm in this relationship until I get bored with it, or until it becomes inconvenient, or until something better comes along." Lack of commitment cheapens the relationship.

More marriages end in divorce for people who have lived together before marriage than for those who haven't. Several estimates rate the failure rate of marriage at 80 to 85 percent among those who have lived together before marrying.[4] Couples move in together to have a trial marriage. The fact that it is a trial and not a covenant relationship sows the seed of defeat. Living together doesn't give couples any idea of what it is going to be like to be married to their partner. When commitment is brought into the picture, it's a whole different relationship.

A young woman, a member of a Lutheran church, was confronted by her pastor about her live-in boyfriend. She defended herself by saying, "It saves on expenses." By living together and having sex, she and her live-in boyfriend didn't have to pay two separate rents. When the pastor told her it was prostitution, she became enraged. "I'm not a prostitute!" she screamed. Yet that is exactly what God condemned when he inspired the holy authors of the Bible to use the word "prostitution" to describe sex for any kind of consideration. It took an excommunication to bring home a reality forgotten today by many churches.

> Israel, what does the Lord your God want you to do? He wants you to fear him, follow all his directions, love him, and worship him with all your heart and with all your soul. The Lord wants you to obey his commands and laws that I'm giving you today for your own good. (Deut.10:12–13)

God knows what works and what doesn't work for us because he created us. He knows what makes us emotionally, physically, and spiritually whole and healthy. When we, as Christians, engage in the sin of fornication, a form of prostitution, we're trying to live with one foot in the world and its so-called pleasures and the other foot in God's kingdom. It can't be done. It's like standing on a partially frozen pond with each foot on a separate sheet of ice. As one piece moves to the left and the other to the right, it becomes increasingly uncomfortable. Eventually we're going to have to place both feet on a single sheet of ice because the ice is moving in different directions. We *must* choose between the world and God, and we already know which one leads to present and eternal joy. Choosing the world leads to eternal destruction.

Some readers will nod their heads in agreement when reading about other hell-bound sinners throughout this book, but when they get to this section on fornicators, they will disregard it, their minds having already been polluted by society's view of fornication. That's really sad and unfortunate. God hasn't changed. His Word hasn't changed. We have become accepting and tolerant of sins God abhors and which do not lead to true happiness for anyone.

There are those who will say, "But I'm faithful to God in all other areas of my life. Surely he wouldn't condemn me to hell just for having sex with my girlfriend." God's ways are *not* our ways. The Bible says we are condemned because we have not trusted Jesus. (John 3:16–19)

> If someone obeys all God's laws except one, that person is guilty of breaking all of them. After all, the one who said, "Never commit adultery," is the same one who said, "Never murder." If you do not commit adultery but you murder, you become a person who disobeys God's laws. (James 2:10–11)

And by the same token, if you do not commit murder but commit adultery or fornication, you become a person who disobeys God's laws. I find it astonishing that some of the same Christians who publicly condemn homosexuality, because God's Word says it's wrong, continue to engage in the sin of fornication. God has said both sins are disgusting to him, and he doesn't see homosexuality as being any worse than adultery, fornication, or other sins which he has proclaimed will be punished by eternal death. Sin is about the condition of the heart. Only those whose hearts have been changed by the new birth (being born again) can be faithful to God. They do not want any sin in their lives.

Those who engage in what is loosely called "premarital sex" should realize it is a sin to be punished with eternal damnation. You can't claim to be a Christian and then claim you don't understand how God views covenant marriage. He created sexual and emotional intimacy to happen only within that context. No matter how large a percentage of society decides premarital sex isn't wrong, what God has to say about it will be all that matters on judgment day. God says fornicators can't enter the kingdom of heaven.

The almost married

An elderly woman decided to live with her boyfriend, rather than marry him, because she would no longer receive her deceased husband's pension and social security benefits if she were to remarry. Her fear isn't based on faith or love. Yes, she would pay a financial penalty if she married her boyfriend, but faith in Jesus knows God will provide for those who do what's right.

Another elderly couple also feared a financial loss should they marry, but they wanted to enter into a marriage covenant. They participated in a wedding ceremony and exchanged vows, but they didn't turn in any of the government paperwork that would qualify them as being legally married in the eyes of the state and thus subject them to the so-called "marriage penalty."

They too are cowards, as well as thieves, living in fear of financial loss, not paying their legal share of taxes, and not trusting God to provide for them. In not getting legally married, this couple is showing unbelief. Fear draws us away from God and causes us to lose the blessings he bestows on those who are obedient to him. Obviously money is the consideration here, and God calls that fornication/prostitution as well.

Media influence

One of the biggest factors influencing our biblical views of adultery and fornication over the past fifty years is the media. When we constantly read about or view situations in which adultery and fornication, as well as other sexual sins, are accepted and even encouraged, we convince ourselves that these sins must be okay because "everyone's doing it." Everyone wasn't engaging in adultery until the media placed its seal of approval on the sins.

We should stop purchasing magazines that portray adultery and fornication in a positive light, and we should stop viewing television programs, movies, and Internet sites that glorify sexual sins. When the media promotes sins the Bible says lead only to death and destruction, and we willingly view these sins, we allow the devil an entrance into our hearts and into our lives. It might start with a thought or a lust and lead to more damaging behavior. The only way to avoid falling prey to Satan's temptations through the media is to completely avoid those magazines and shows that allow the thoughts and ideas of sexual immorality to grow and fester in our hearts.

All who have accepted Jesus as their Lord and Savior are in various stages of yielding their will and their life to him. The question of whether we are in rebellion to God or not is this: Do we *know* what we're doing is wrong? God looks at our hearts. If we know we're being disobedient but go ahead and do what we want, we are in rebellion, and that's what sin is: rebellion against God.

If in your heart you know you need to and are ready to repent of adultery or fornication and ask for God's grace and mercy won through Jesus' blood shed on the cross, you can say this prayer.

Dear Father, please forgive me for committing the sin of adultery/fornication. I am sincerely sorry for my sins and know that Jesus' blood shed on the cross has cleansed me of all unrighteousness. Please help me as I go about restoring my marriage and remain faithful to my spouse/please help me as I abstain from sex until I'm married. Give me the courage to make my marriage legal in your eyes and in the eyes of the state. I accept Jesus as my Lord and Savior and look forward to the day when he will return and take me and all believers to heaven to live with you forever in your glorious kingdom. In Jesus' name I pray. Amen.

2

The Cowards

The Lord is my light and my salvation. Who is there to fear? The Lord is my life's fortress. Who is there to be afraid of? (Ps. 27:1)

*Debbie witnessed the abuse of her neighbor's two young children on an almost daily basis. She cried frequently for the plight of the young boys and prayed for their safety, but she felt helpless to do anything about the situation. She refused to call Child Protection Services for fear her neighbor would learn who had called and retaliate. Debbie is a coward, not doing what she knows the Lord wants her to do because she doesn't believe God will keep her safe.

The Bible tells us the cowardly will not enter heaven. Why cowards? How do they hurt anyone just by being afraid? Cowards show they don't truly know God because they don't rely on him as their provider, protector, and Savior. Regardless of what they *say* they believe, their actions indicate habitual unbelief. To love God means to fear, love, obey, and trust him.

> You fool! Do you have to be shown that faith which does nothing is useless? (James 2:20)

Living in fear

*Dorothy is so afraid someone will break into her home that she has added two extra locks to her front and back doors and has nailed her windows shut. She doesn't carry a purse for fear it will give a thief a reason to rob her, and she carries a small container of mace with her whenever she ventures out. She lives her life in constant fear of being harmed.

There is nothing wrong with safeguarding our homes and wanting to protect ourselves and our property, but it is a sin to live in fear. Jesus said, "Fear not." God's love cannot be made perfect in us if we constantly worry or if we are afraid of people or situations. It is no coincidence that the phrase "Fear not" appears 365 times in the Bible, once for every day of the year.

> We have known and believed that God loves us. God is love. Those who live in God's love live in God, and God lives in them. God's love has reached its goal in us. So we look ahead with confidence to the day of judgment. While we are in this world, we are exactly like him with regard to love. No fear exists where his love is. Rather, perfect love gets rid of fear, because fear involves punishment. The person who lives in fear doesn't have perfect love. (1 John 4:16–18)

You can turn your life over to fear, or you can turn your life over to God, but not both. Satan wants you to be afraid. He wants to keep you living in fear about your life now and after death. He knows that when you're afraid, you are in a state of unbelief, that you are not trusting God. God wants us to trust him and his promises, both for the earthly life and for the life to come.

Our battle–hardened champion is Jesus, who fought the battle against sin, death, and Satan. When we place our trust in Jesus, the Holy Spirit is always working in our hearts, filling us more and more with the ability to know God's love, which casts out *all* fear. Faith in this life means that no matter what circumstances or difficulties we face, we are called to trust our Lord Jesus because he has defeated the worst enemies imaginable. For the life to come, we trust that Jesus' innocent blood shed for us covers our sin and enables us to stand before Holy God.

If you truly have faith, then you will trust with your whole heart that God is with you at all times. Nothing happens to you that he does not allow to happen. When he does allow something bad to happen to you, then he will stay with you. He will use the trial to refine and grow you, and he will bring you out of the situation better off than when you went into it. You will go through difficult times, because trials are part of life, but Jesus has promised never to leave you or forsake you. Remember, Jesus said, "Don't be afraid of those who kill the body but cannot kill the soul. Instead, fear the one who can destroy both body and soul in hell." (Matt. 10:28) Having recovered from a stoning where his opponents thought they had killed him, Paul said: "We must suffer a lot to enter the kingdom of God." (Acts 14:22)

We are cowards when we cringe at the thought of terrorists or Bird Flu or anyone or anything that has the possibility of harming us. If we truly believe Jesus has triumphed over sin, death, and hell, then we will trust him and be at peace with the world around us.

> You, O Lord, are my refuge! You have made the Most High your home. No harm will come to you. No sickness will come near your house. He will put his angels in charge of you to protect you in all your ways. They will carry you in their hands so that you never hit your foot against a rock. You will step on lions and cobras. You will trample young lions and snakes. (Ps. 91:9–13)

My neighbor's dog, Kirby, spends his mornings tied to a long leash in front of his house. At least several times a week, while chasing after a bird or squirrel, the dog gets himself so tangled in his leash that all he can do is lie on the ground and wait to be rescued. Despite his predicament, Kirby always remains happy and calm, his tail occasionally thumping on the ground when someone passes by. His serenity is easily explained: He doesn't want to whine and draw the attention of his owner, who will make him go back inside for awhile, and he has learned from experience that someone will soon notice he's tangled in his leash again and will grant him his freedom.

Despite what must be a terrifying experience to a dog, Kirby is neither worried nor afraid. If only we could be as brave as this young dog when we are in what might seem to be a hopeless situation, but panic strikes and we rely on our own wits, impulsively doing things to make the situation worse. We are cowards, not trusting and relying on God to see us through difficult times. Our Master will always come to the rescue when we cry out to him.

> Turn all your anxiety over to God because he cares for you. Keep your mind clear and be alert. Your opponent the devil is prowling around like a roaring lion as he looks for someone to devour. (1 Pet. 5:7–8)

We all have moments when we forget the Lord is our shield of protection. Even Abraham had his cowardly moments. When facing a severe famine, he took his wife Sarah and went to Egypt. Fearful that the Egyptians would kill him and take his wife, a very beautiful woman, Abraham told Sarah to lie to the Egyptians and say she was his sister. As a result, Sarah was taken to Pharaoh's palace by his officials.

Abraham was a coward and a liar, not trusting God to protect him and his wife if he told the Egyptians the truth. God was angered by Abraham's cowardliness and struck Pharaoh and his household with terrible plagues because of Sarah. When the Lord afflicted Pharaoh and his household, Abraham's deception was discovered. He got himself and others into a real mess by trying to rely on his own wits rather than trusting God to protect him and his family. Abraham's cowardice had a profound effect on those around him. (Gen. 20:1–18)

Choosing to worry

Cowards can also be found in the way of worriers. *Myrtle worries constantly. Will she have a ride to church on Sunday morning? Will she have enough money to pay her bills this month? Will the vacant apartment next to her be rented to someone who stays up late watching television on full volume? She is a coward, worrying about things she has no control over and not putting all her circumstances in God's hands. God knows she needs a ride to church. He knows she has bills to pay. He knows who would make the best neighbor for her, and it may just be the guy who plays his television loud. If we put our trust in God, we may not always get what we think we want, but we will always get what God knows is best for us.

> Jesus said, "So I tell you to stop worrying about what you will eat, drink, or wear. Isn't life more than food and the body more than clothes? Look at the birds. They don't plant, harvest, or gather the harvest into barns. Yet your heavenly Father feeds them. Aren't you worth more than they? Can any of you add a single hour to your life by worrying? And why worry about clothes? Notice how the flowers grow in the field. They never work or spin yarn for clothes. But I say that not even Solomon in all his majesty was dressed like one of these flowers. That's the way God clothes the grass in the field. Today it's alive, and tomorrow it's thrown into an incinerator. So how much more will he clothe you people who have so little faith? Don't ever worry and say, 'What are we going to eat?' or 'What are we going to drink?' or 'What are we going to wear?' Everyone is concerned about these things, and your heavenly Father certainly knows you need all of them. But first, be concerned about his kingdom and what has his approval. Then all these things will be provided for you. So don't ever worry about tomorrow. After all, tomorrow will worry about itself. Each day has enough trouble of its own." (Matt. 6:25–34)

It is a sin to worry. If we worry about how we'll pay rent or buy groceries for the week or whether we'll be laid off from our jobs, we have not turned our will and our life over to God. God knows we need all these things, and he'll take care of us. When we don't trust him to take care of us and to provide for us, we disown him; we live in a state of unbelief. When judgment day comes, he will say he doesn't know us because we didn't know, seek, or acknowledge him.

> What will separate us from the love Christ has for us? Can trouble, distress, persecution, hunger, nakedness, danger, or violent death separate us from his love? As scripture says: "We are being killed all day long because of you. We are thought of as sheep to be slaughtered." The one who loves us gives us an

> overwhelming victory in all these difficulties. I am convinced that nothing can ever separate us from God's love which Christ Jesus our Lord shows us. We can't be separated by death or life, by angels or rulers, by anything in the present or anything in the future, by forces or powers in the world above or in the world below, or by anything else in creation. (Rom. 8:35–39)

The opposite of worry and fear is faith—absolute trust in the Lord. If you have faith, you are secure in the Lord as your shield of protection and as your provider. I've heard it said that faith is the ability not to panic. What reason would you ever have to panic in any situation when God is your protector?

> Even when I am afraid, I still trust you. I praise the word of God. I trust God. I am not afraid. What can mere flesh and blood do to me? (Ps. 56:3–4)

Parents who worry about their children to the extent that they want to control all or most aspects of their children's lives are cowards. They are saying to God, "I don't trust you to protect my children." Children raised by parents who are cowards often grow to be cowards themselves.

A neighbor still persists in trying to control her adult children, both of whom are in their forties. When her son married a few years ago, she argued with him about who he could and could not invite to his own wedding, which he was paying for himself. She threatened she would not attend the wedding if he refused to honor her wishes about who should not be on the wedding list.

Another woman, in her ultimate battle for financial control over her children's lives, has included a condition in her will stating that their inheritance would be placed in a trust to be distributed to her middle-age "kids" a few thousand dollars per year. She wants to continue to be able to control them even after she's dead!

Whether we are trying to control our own lives or someone else's, the desire for control alienates us from God. God can't possibly be in control when we're trying to control everything ourselves. Cowards are afraid that allowing God to control a situation won't result in the outcome they want, even though his outcome is guaranteed to be what's best for everyone involved.

Many elderly people and others, unfortunately, have stopped voting for political candidates who oppose abortion, homosexual marriage, and who stand up for morals and values. Voters worry that they might lose their social security benefits, or that the job market will suffer, or that they won't have adequate health coverage, among other things, if they don't vote for the candidate who campaigns for these issues rather than the candidate who campaigns for restoring values. Some simply cast a vote for the candidate their union endorses, regardless of that candidate's values.

We should always support political candidates we believe Jesus would most likely vote for if he were voting in an election, and then trust God to provide everything else we need. We can't let those who promote things God calls sin frighten us into supporting their agendas based on fear. We can't be cowardly when we go to the polls and then complain about what a shame it is that the morals and values of today are so much lower than they were fifty years ago. We are the ones who are causing the sinking values when we cowardly cast a vote for health benefits or job creation rather than values!

Regardless of how we vote, we have a duty as Christians and as citizens to be at our designated polling places on election day to vote. President Calvin Coolidge said, "I urge all the voters of our country, without reference to party, that they assemble tomorrow at their respective voting places in the exercise of the high office of American citizenship, that they approach the ballot box in the spirit that they would approach a sacrament. Make choice of public officers solely in the light of conscience. When an election is so held ... it sustains the belief that the voice of the people is the voice of God."[1]

Confessing our faith

Worry is only half the story on cowards. God considers those who are afraid to publicly confess their faith in him to be cowards too. Those who are afraid they'll be embarrassed or that they'll lose their jobs, friends, homes, families, or even their lives if they confess Jesus is Lord are cowards.

The Apostle Paul faced death for publicly stating that Jesus is the Son of God; he suffered beatings, being thrown in jail, shipwreck, and ultimately was killed because of his faith in the Lord. Paul trusted God to protect him as he spread the gospel until the appointed time for him to die. He said, "To be absent from the body is to be present in the Lord."

While going through many trials, Paul rejoiced that he was able to share in Christ's sufferings because he realized he would be gaining a great heavenly reward. We too must confess Jesus Christ is Lord of our lives and spread the gospel at every opportunity without fearing the reaction of other people.

> Jesus said: So I will acknowledge in front of my Father in heaven that person who acknowledges me in front of others. But I will tell my Father in heaven that I don't know the person who tells others that he doesn't know me. (Matt. 10:32–33)

Cowards are those who don't stand up for the oppressed and demand justice. The kid in school who sees someone being bullied but never says anything or gets help is a coward. The person who hears the Lord's name used as a curse word at work but never objects is a coward. The person who witnesses something unjust but doesn't do anything is a coward.

In a fit of road rage, a young man from Detroit stripped the clothes from a driver who had bumped into him in traffic and pummeled her with a tire iron for ten minutes. To get away from him, the woman jumped off a bridge to her death. Over forty people witnessed the attack, yet not one stepped in to restrain him or to rescue the woman.[2]

An elderly woman took a train to visit her mother. While riding the train, two prostitutes and a pimp subjected her to verbal and physical abuse. They blew smoke in her face, dropped burning cigarettes into her lap, and poured beer over her head. She looked around at other passengers, her eyes pleading with them to help her, but the other passengers just looked away. When she was exiting the train, several men patted her on the back and told her how brave she had been through her ordeal. Not one passenger came to her rescue.[3]

When two-year-old James Bulger was abducted from a mall by two ten-year-old boys and was tortured, beaten, and placed on railway tracks, thirty-eight people saw the boys during their two-mile journey to the tracks. Several witnesses said later they had noticed Bulger was bruised and bleeding, but none stepped in to help the toddler during his death march.[4] Irish Statesman Edmund Burke said, "All that is necessary for the triumph of evil is that good men do nothing." These people and many others might be alive today if a few good men had intervened.

It isn't just during violent acts that we show cowardice. Our apathy goes much further. We must speak out in love when a few unbelievers want to remove God's name from our currency. We must write to or call our congressmen when unbelievers try to remove God's name from our national pledge. We must reveal God's Word about homosexuality when unbelievers want to change state laws to allow homosexuals to marry. We must hate the sin but love the sinner as we boldly stand up for Jesus and attempt to save our country from God's wrath. We must stop being cowards!

Christiana Sewell of Colorado Springs is not a coward. Several months before voters of the state of Colorado were to decide whether or not to accept domestic partnerships, Sewell placed signs in her front yard, expressing her opinion that marriage should be between one man and one woman. Homosexual activists had been placing signs around the neighborhood which pictured a dog saying, "Moo," trying to persuade voters that homosexuals are just "born different."

Sewell placed a sign which pictured a dog saying, "Woof," telling voters dogs don't moo, and homosexuals can stop their sexually immoral behavior with God's help. A person opposed to Sewell's signs stole them and left a threatening letter in their place. Sewell put out more signs. The thief continued to steal the signs, and Sewell continued to replace them. The vandals then dragged a trashcan onto Sewell's lawn and set the signs on fire. Despite Sewell's fear that those who had been claiming to promote "tolerance" and "diversity" were now capable of burning down her house or injuring her children, she once again displayed more signs on her lawn shortly after the fire had been extinguished. She refused to back down in her efforts to exercise her right to freedom of religious speech.[5]

Megan Chapman is not a coward. She stood at her Russell County High School graduation and shared with classmates how Jesus Christ had changed her life. Three hours prior to the graduation ceremony, Chapman had been threatened with a lawsuit by the American Civil Liberties Union (ACLU) if she prayed at the ceremony. With the real threat of being charged with a crime looming, Chapman boldly confessed her faith in her Lord and Savior Jesus Christ, and 200 brave graduates joined her in reciting the Lord's Prayer.[6]

Michael Marcavage, president of Repent America, is not a coward. He expressed his outrage at a play depicting Jesus as a homosexual being shown at Temple University and was escorted to a mental ward for his protest. Some time later, as he addressed the Lansdowne Borough council meeting and began reading from the Bible, he was arrested by the police chief for "hate speech" and charged with disrupting a meeting and disorderly conduct. More recently, he was arrested and charged with a "hate crime" in Philadelphia for reading from the Bible at a homosexual rally.[7]

Dianne Haskett, former mayor of London in Ontario, Canada, is not a coward. Haskett was fined $10,000 when she refused to proclaim a gay pride weekend. She resigned as mayor rather than proclaim an event which promoted sinful behavior.[8]

Tim Bono, owner of Bono Film and Video in Arlington, Virginia, is not a coward. When a woman presented videos depicting homosexuality to Bono and asked that he copy them for her, he refused. The woman filed a complaint with the local Human Rights Commission, which told Bono he must either copy the videos for the woman or pay to have someone else copy them. Bono again refused, despite threats of losing his business license for discriminating on the basis of sexual orientation.[9]

Actor Stephen Baldwin is not a coward. He is doing everything he can to prevent a sex shop from opening in his community in Nyack, New York. The shop plans to have at least eight video booths available for patrons to view pornography. Baldwin has voiced his objections to the media, has spoken to the city council, and has threatened to post photographs and license plate numbers of the sex shop's customers on the Internet.[10]

President George W. Bush is probably the best example of someone who isn't afraid to publicly confess his faith and to make many decisions based on biblical principles, which is probably why he is hated around the world. He may have been one of the people Jesus was referring to when he said, "All nations will hate you because of me." (Matt. 24:9) President Bush is a brave man. Despite having insults hurled at him by liberals, the media, and foreign nations, he continues to stand firm in his faith regardless of opinion polls.

> Blessed are you when people insult you, persecute you, lie, and say all kinds of evil things about you because of me. Rejoice and be glad because you have a great reward in heaven! The prophets who lived before you were persecuted in these ways. (Matt. 5:11–12)

In America, we still have the freedom to preach the gospel of Jesus Christ to others, and we should take advantage of that freedom while it still exists. In the not too distant future it could be considered "hate speech" to warn others about hell. If we don't proclaim Jesus now, while it costs us very little, will we be ready to do it when it may cost us a lot? In many countries, preaching Christianity can result in death.

In North Korea, following Jesus is considered treason, punishable by imprisonment or even death. In China, Christians' Bibles are confiscated and they face prison sentences and fines for worshipping Jesus. According to the *Voice of the Martyrs* Web site, a man known only as Evangelist Daniel is serving a five–year prison term in Indonesia for praying. Father Nguyen Van Ly is serving an eight–year prison term in Viet Nam for criticizing the government's persecution of Christians. Pastor Shestakov is serving four years in a labor camp in Uzbekisten for proselytizing. Pastor Wang Weillang and eleven others are serving from one to three and a half years in a China prison for praying and reading the Bible. Pastor Van Thong and eleven others in the Lao People's Democratic Republic were arrested in November 2006 for attending meetings arranged by Christians from the West. They are denied visitors and are being held indefinitely. Ms. Li Yang was arrested in China in 2001 for editing a Christian publication. She is serving a fifteen–year sentence.[11]

Being Jesus' disciple may cost you something, but your heavenly destiny is worth far more than anything you could give up in this life. Those afraid to obey are the cowards. Jesus said those willing to lose their lives will find them, and those who find their lives must lose them. What can anyone do to you when God is your protector? Absolutely nothing that is not within God's will for you. If you're a worrier or someone who is always fearful, you are probably one of the cowards God talks about when he says,

> The cowardly will find themselves in the fiery lake of burning sulfur. (Rev. 21:8)

Witnessing to others

The most important thing we can do as Christians is tell others about our salvation won through Jesus Christ. Some Christians live their entire lives without ever sharing the good news of Jesus' death and resurrection with even one other person! And yet the way Jesus went about getting people to change their behaviors was to change their hearts by telling them the good news of God's love.

Suppose your child's teacher tells you your child is having difficulty at school, and she believes the reason is because he can't see very well. You are going to go out that very day and have his eyes checked. If the new glasses help him to see more clearly and, as a result, his grades improve, you will rejoice in his success.

There are many people around you, such as neighbors, co-workers, family members, and friends, who can't see clearly that salvation has been won for them by Jesus Christ. It is your responsibility, as a disciple of Christ, to share the gospel message with them and to open their eyes to the truth. It is the cowards who are afraid to witness to others. All you have to do is plant the seed of salvation in their heart. The Holy Spirit will help their faith to grow.

Rev. Brad Aldrich, a Lutheran minister, believes witnessing is so important he has given up his job and the opportunity to minister at a church and instead travels around the country training people how to tell others about Jesus. His CD, *Witness Boldly, Confidently, and Naturally without Offending Your Hearers*, can be purchased at www.crosspollinationministries.com. The CD will tell you exactly how to approach a friend or stranger and talk to them about Jesus. According to Aldrich, nine out of ten people welcome the gospel message when using his biblical method of witnessing.

Money

Cowards don't tithe (give 10 percent of their income to God). Tithing and giving offerings show trust in the Lord as your provider. If your reason for not tithing is because you're worried you won't have enough money to make ends meet, then you are not trusting God to care for you. Many people are afraid of how they will be able to pay all their bills if they tithe. That fear doesn't come from God; it comes from Satan or the sinful flesh we still carry with us. Satan wants you to be afraid to tithe and to give offerings as the Holy Spirit directs because he doesn't want you to receive the blessings that come from trusting and obeying the Lord. (*For more on tithing, see Chapter Seventeen: Thieves.*)

Cowards are afraid to give and to share. They will say they can't afford to give, even when they have more than they need right now, because they may need it in the future. God is a now God. He gives us our "daily bread" and wants us to trust him for the future. When God provided the Israelites with manna in the wilderness each morning, he wanted them to take only what they could eat that day. He told them not to store food for the future because he wanted them to trust that he would provide for them each day. In the same manner, he wants us to trust that we can cheerfully present our tithes to him without worrying about how we'll be able to pay for all the necessities of daily living.

If in your heart you know you need to and are ready to repent of being cowardly and receive God's forgiveness, you can say this prayer.

Dear Father, please forgive me for being cowardly. I understand now that I have not truly believed in you or in your Son Jesus. Forgive me for worrying and being fearful of things when I know you have everything under control in my life. Help me to put my full trust in you so I can live my life joyfully and trustingly as a giver. Help me to stand up for what is right, and to be bold enough to proclaim my faith in you to other people. I declare Jesus is my Lord and Savior and look forward to the day when he will return to take me and all believers to heaven to live with you forever in your glorious kingdom. In Jesus' name I pray. Amen.

3

The Disobedient Christians

We are sure that we know Christ if we obey his commandments. The person who says, "I know him," but doesn't obey his commandments is a liar. The truth isn't in that person. But whoever obeys what Christ says is the kind of person in whom God's love is perfected. That's how we know we are in Christ. Those who say that they live in him must live the same way he lived. (1 John 2:3–6)

Though *Laurie was baptized as an infant and was brought up in a church, at age seventeen she decided she wanted to have a baby, so she had sex and became pregnant. A couple of years later, she became pregnant again. She has been living with her boyfriend for several years and has no plans to marry.

Church–goers *Lloyd and *Grace have made a small fortune investing in real estate. They give a weekly offering of ten to twenty dollars, less than 1 percent of their income, and they give every now and then when there's a national disaster.

*Jeff was raised in a Christian home and school. He hangs out at bars, frequently gets drunk, and smokes an occasional joint. He no longer attends church.

*Gerry is a minister in the Episcopal church. He preaches about Jesus Christ, but he lives with another man and professes to be a homosexual. He also abuses alcohol.

All of these people believe they are destined for heaven because they "believe in Jesus," but the way they live indicates they don't know Jesus the Christ and that the Great Exchange hasn't happened in their lives. In effect, they have said, "God, I'll obey some of your commands, but I think you're wrong about these other things." Laurie, Lloyd, Grace, Jeff, and Gerry are all in danger on judgment day of hearing Jesus say, "I don't know you."

> Be careful, brothers and sisters, that none of you ever develop a wicked, unbelieving heart that turns away from the living God. Encourage each other every day while you have the opportunity. If you do this, none of you will be deceived by sin and become stubborn. After all, we will remain Christ's part-

ners only if we continue to hold on to our original confidence until the end. Scripture says, "If you hear God speak today, don't be stubborn. Don't be stubborn like those who rebelled." Who heard God and rebelled? All those whom Moses led out of Egypt rebelled. With whom was God angry for 40 years? He was angry with those who sinned and died in the desert. Who did God swear would never enter his place of rest? He was talking about those who didn't obey him. So we see that they couldn't enter his place of rest because they didn't believe. (Heb. 3:12–18)

Disobedience has a price

Many who call themselves Christians will not inherit the kingdom of God. Disobedient Christians are those who *say* they believe Jesus is the Son of God, that he died to forgive their sins, that he rose from the dead and sent his Holy Spirit to live in us and enable us to lead lives pleasing to him, and that he will return one day to judge both the living and the dead. Their lives, however, show they don't actually believe this at all. They don't understand and have not actually made the Great Exchange. To really believe in Jesus means to make him Lord of your life. You no longer live for yourself but for him, by faith in him and in his Word, and with the power of the Holy Spirit working in your heart, which produces visible change. Understand that you cannot pick and choose what you like from God's Word, the Bible, because Jesus *is* the Word. Churches are overflowing with disobedient Christians.

> Do what God's word says. Don't merely listen to it, or you will fool yourselves. If someone listens to God's word but doesn't do what it says, he is like a person who looks at his face in a mirror, studies his features, goes away, and immediately forgets what he looks like. However, the person who continues to study God's perfect teachings that make people free and who remains committed to them will be blessed. People like that don't merely listen and forget; they actually do what God's teachings say. (James 1:22–25)

When God gave the teachings, including the Ten Commandments, to Moses, he said if we obey his instructions, he will be our God, and we will be blessed. God also told Moses not only will we be blessed for following his instructions, but we will be cursed for disobeying his instructions.

> Today I'm giving you the choice of a blessing or a curse. You'll be blessed if you obey the commands of the Lord your God that I'm giving you today. You'll be cursed if you disobey the commands of the Lord your God, if you

turn from the way I'm commanding you to live today, and if you worship other gods you never knew. (Deut.11:26–28)

God's commands

God's commands are summed up in Matthew 22:37–40: Jesus [said] "'Love the Lord your God with all your heart, with all your soul, and with all your mind.' This is the greatest and most important commandment. The second is like it; 'Love your neighbor as you love yourself.' All of Moses' Teachings and the Prophets depend on these two commandments."

God knew we could not perfectly obey his commands because of our sinful nature. That's why he sent Jesus, God the Son, the God–man in human flesh. Jesus took our place and received the punishment we deserved. Then he rose from the dead and went back to heaven, sending his Holy Spirit to live and work in those who believe in him. With the Great Exchange, exchanging your life for Christ's, obedience is possible.

God gave his commandments for our own good, to protect us, and also to prepare us for our eternal destiny where the obedient now will continue to live with him on the new earth. He also gave them so his people, the ones who trust in him and willingly try to obey him, would show his love, faithfulness, and glory. We could not perfectly live according to his revealed will in the Ten Commandments, so he sent his Spirit to live and work in us. In the Great Exchange, we receive his Spirit to work his character and his nature in us. As we are changed in the Great Ex*change*, the Bible says his instructions are written on all hearts so that when we are endowed with his Holy Spirit, we will *want* to obey him.

One of Satan's favorite lies is that obeying God is boring and that if we obey God, we will lose our unique identity. Actually the opposite is true. Living by faith is a daily adventure, and it is the devil who tries to get everybody to conform and to do what everyone else is doing. God created us as unique, irreplaceable individuals—not interchangeable—and it is in following Jesus that we find our true individuality and God's unique plan for our lives. God is creative; Satan is not.

> If we go on sinning after we have learned the truth, no sacrifice can take away our sins. All that is left is a terrifying wait for judgment and a raging fire that will consume God's enemies. If two or three witnesses accused someone of rejecting Moses' Teachings, that person was shown no mercy as he was executed. What do you think a person who shows no respect for the Son of God deserves? That person looks at the blood of the promise (the blood that made him holy) as no different from other people's blood, and he insults the Spirit

that God gave us out of his kindness. He deserves a much worse punishment. (Heb. 10:26–29)

Human beings are much happier when they are not drinking or drugging to numb pain or just to get high. Humans are also much happier when they're not seeking love in all the wrong places, such as fornicating and committing adultery, stealing from others, coveting a neighbor's possessions, or gossiping, just to name a few destructive behaviors. God wants us to receive peace, joy, and heavenly training as we focus on following him and willingly obeying his instructions.

> This is what the Lord, your Defender, the Holy One of Israel, says: I am the Lord your God. I teach you what is best for you. I lead you where you should go. If only you had listened to my commands! Your peace would be like a river that never runs dry. Your righteousness would be like waves on the sea. Your descendants would be like sand. Your children would be like its grains. Their names would not be cut off or wiped out in my presence. (Is. 48:17–19)

Peace through obedience

Can you truthfully say you go through life with your heart at peace no matter what the circumstances look like? That's what Jesus came to provide for you, and you can claim it through faith, trust, and obedience. In being obedient Christians, we can't pick and choose which of God's commands we are going to obey. He tells us to obey *all* his commands. If there is even one of God's commands we're ignoring, then we are being disobedient. For our fleshly nature, this is impossible, as Paul writes in Romans 7:14. But with the exchange of Christ's life for ours, the Holy Spirit empowers us to live in a way that pleases God. (Romans 8:1–17)

Many Christians are disobedient by withholding their tithes and offerings from God. God may say on judgment day, "You treasure money more than me." Other Christians are disobedient in their use of alcohol or drugs, still others with their lying, gossiping, adultery, or homosexual behavior.

Now let's be clear—salvation isn't based on what you do; it's based on what Jesus did for you. Good works won't earn you a ticket to heaven; only Jesus' blood can give you that. But obedience and good works are the *sign* that the Great Exchange has taken place—you live Christ's life, not your own.

> When I tried to obey the law's standards, those laws killed me. As a result, I live in a relationship with God. I have been crucified with Christ. I no longer

live, but Christ lives in me. The life I now live I live by believing in God's Son, who loved me and took the punishment for my sins. (Gal. 2:19–20)

If your heart has been changed by God, then you will delight in obeying his commands, and you will trust him to take care of you, your family, and all your needs as you allow him to reach out to others through you. You will want to please God, and you won't be worrying about your circumstances.

> Because you are children who obey God, don't live the kind of life you once lived. Once you lived to satisfy your desires because you didn't know any better. But because the God who called you is holy, you must be holy in every aspect of your life. (1 Pet.1:14–15)

> You unfaithful people! Don't you know that love for this evil world is hatred toward God? Whoever wants to be a friend of this world is an enemy of God. (James 4:4)

Faith through obedience

When people were disobedient during Noah's day, God wiped them off the face of the earth, saving only Noah and his family. When Jonah disobeyed God, he was swallowed by a large fish, where he remained for three days until he repented and came into obedience. When the people living in Sodom and Gomorrah were disobedient, God completely destroyed them and the cities in which they lived. Thanks be to God we have Jesus, who died so that we could be forgiven and have the opportunity to come into obedience to God's commands through the heart-changing power of the Holy Spirit.

> The corrupt nature's attitude leads to death. But the spiritual nature's attitude leads to life and peace. This is so because the corrupt nature has a hostile attitude toward God. It refuses to place itself under the authority of God's standards because it can't. Those who are under the control of the corrupt nature can't please God. But if God's Spirit lives in you, you are under the control of your spiritual nature, not your corrupt nature. (Rom. 8:6–9)

Obedience comes from faith, which means we *live* as though what we say we believe is true. We believe God loves us and has given his instructions for our own good, and we believe we have a wonderful eternal future in heaven, so we follow him! When we have faith God will care for us and protect us, we can trust that his will for our lives is going to be what is best for us. When we don't obey

God, we're telling him we don't trust him; we trust ourselves to run our lives better than he can.

> You were taught to change the way you were living. The person you used to be will ruin you through desires that deceive you. However, you were taught to have a new attitude. You were also taught to become a new person to be like God, truly righteous and holy. (Eph. 4:24)

When God told Abraham to offer his beloved son Isaac as a sacrifice, Abraham never questioned God. Not once did he say, "What?! You want me to kill my one and only son whom I love?" Abraham didn't even ask God *why* he wanted him to kill his young son. He simply obeyed, trusting and knowing God always knows best and had his and Isaac's best interests in mind. He believed that God would raise Isaac from the dead so God's promise that Abraham would be the father of many nations would come true. Abraham was living his life for God, not for Isaac, his wife, or anyone else.

When Abraham tied up Isaac and was about to plunge the knife into the boy's chest, God stopped him. God didn't want innocent blood shed; God wanted complete obedience. Abraham's willingness to be obedient to God despite his own wishes pleased God, and he blessed Abraham abundantly throughout his life. (Gen. 22:1–14)

Disobedient Christians

Disobedient Christians claim Jesus' name but don't live for him, so their lives don't portray him as he really is. They don't show his faithfulness, his love, or his holiness. Some say God doesn't care about sin and that no one will go to hell. Wouldn't it make you angry if people were lying about you and putting people's souls in danger? The Bible says God prefers people to be *for* him or *against* him; God can work in the hearts of passionate people.

> Jesus said, I know what you have done, that you are neither cold nor hot. I wish you were cold or hot. But since you are lukewarm and not hot or cold, I'm going to spit you out of my mouth. (Rev. 3:15–16)

A minister of a large evangelical church presents the perfect profile of a disobedient Christian. He had served the Lord by preaching the saving message of the gospel and seemed to be the perfect disciple, even traveling the country preaching against homosexual behavior. He was recently fired from his position, however, after a male prostitute announced to the media that the minister had been having sex with him for the past three years. The minister wrote a letter to his congregation, telling them he was sorry and calling himself "a deceiver and a liar."[1]

This minister needs to fully admit his sin and hypocricy, deal with his pride and self–justification, and repent before the Lord so that he can receive God's forgiveness and move forward in his walk with the Lord. If he has already submitted himself to mentoring and accountability to other brother ministers, then this demonstrates repentance.

Another minister in the Episcopal Church asserts that homosexual behavior is not a sin, that it is not immoral for churches to ordain homosexual ministers, that evolution rather than intelligent design should be taught in schools, and that Jesus is not the only way to heaven. She may call herself a Christian, but she is not following Christ.[2]

These views don't come from God, who created the world and who says homosexual behavior is a sin. Jesus said he is the *only* way to the Father. Ministers who preach these ideas are very dangerous. They are Satan's disciples. They have thrown out most of the Bible and don't really even know the God of the Bible. Their god is a non–existent, politically correct, all–inclusive, tolerant god who will welcome anyone and everyone into heaven. God the Father of Jesus is holy and expects obedience to his Word and his commands, which is the demonstration that we have truly received his Son. We are never to use God's kindness to excuse sin.

The really frightening thing about this particular minister is that her views are heard by thousands and reported by the media. She is leading many, many people who haven't made the Great Exchange down the all–inclusive path to hell. She is using God's kindness and grace as an excuse to engage in sin. God would love for her to turn to him, serve him, and lead lost souls back to him, and hopefully she'll make that choice while it's still an option. If she continues to serve Satan, he's the one with whom she'll be spending eternity.

> Dear friends, I had intended to write to you about the salvation we share. But something has come up. It demands that I write to you and encourage you to continue your fight for the Christian faith that was entrusted to God's holy people once for all time. Some people have slipped in among you unnoticed. Not long ago they were condemned in writing for the following reason: They are people to whom God means nothing. They use God's kindness as an excuse for sexual freedom and deny our only Master and Lord, Jesus Christ. (Jude: 4)

It isn't just ministers who might be considered disobedient or who aren't even really Christians. Others have also rejected Christ after growing up in Christian churches and schools. *Pete, a truck driver in St. Louis, is just one example. Whenever someone tries to talk to Pete about the Lord, he will say, "Yeah, yeah, I know all that stuff." Pete doesn't truly know the Lord or he would know his love and grace and his holiness. He would know God's demand for righteousness and his power to change lives. Jesus is still knocking on the door of Pete's heart, but until Pete answers the door, there is no Great Exchange.

Pete has stopped worshiping the Lord and spends most of his non-working time drinking at a bar. He has turned his back on God, and, come judgment day, the Lord will spit Pete out. He won't inherit the kingdom of heaven unless he repents and comes back into obedience to God's will for his life, which certainly contains far more adventure and satisfaction than sitting around a bar all day. If only Pete would recognize that everything he's trying to find in a bar and never finding can be found in Jesus. If only he would see that everything he's trying to avoid dealing with could be dealt with by Jesus once and for all. Many of us have a "Pete" in our lives, and it is our responsibility to warn them of the consequences of being disobedient Christians.

Obedient Christians

Rev. Jonathan Lange, a Lutheran pastor, is a good example of an obedient Christian. Lange was ministering at Messiah Lutheran Church in St. Louis when St. Paul Lutheran Church in Merced, California, called him to be its pastor. Lange hadn't expressed any interest in receiving another call, nor were his wife and five children interested in leaving their home. All their family and friends were in the St. Louis area, and, after all, Lange had never submitted his name to be placed on a call list.

Surely questions were on their minds. What would they do about his wife's job? She was working for her parents' company, and they needed her. Her parents owned a farm nearby where the family rode their horses and brought children from church to ride. What would they do with their animals? Even if they sold their house, how could they afford a house in California where the cost of living was so much higher? There were so many complications.

The church in California was persistent. They asked Pastor Lange and his wife to please come and visit the congregation and talk with its leaders and members. After the visit, Pastor Lange prayed about the situation and knew God wanted him to go. In obedience to God, he packed up his belongings and moved across the country. His family was to follow after the house sold.

The house went up for sale, and the first couple to look at it bought it. His wife's company was able to find a suitable replacement for her. The Langes have been in California for five years, and God has blessed them with a nice house and acreage for horses and has blessed their new church with growth. Their family is happy and growing in the Lord.

> Then Jesus said to his disciples, "Those who want to come with me must say no to the things they want, pick up their crosses, and follow me. (Matt: 16:24)
>
> If you love me, you will obey my commandments. I will ask the Father, and he will give you another helper who will be with you forever. That helper is the Spirit of Truth. The world cannot accept him because it doesn't see or know him. You know him because he lives with you and will be in you. (John:14:15–17)

A former televangelist, once a disobedient Christian who spent eight years in prison for embezzlement, has answered God's call to serve in love and obedience. He had been criticized and ostracized for having committed adultery.[3]

The televangelist has admitted he sinned but says he discovered God's true identity and will for his life while in prison. He has repented of his sins of pride, greed, and adultery, and has turned back to following Jesus. He has shown that it is possible to turn your life around, to get off the road to hell and back on the path to heaven. He's an inspiration to those who think their sins are so bad or are so many that God won't forgive them. God will forgive our sins for Jesus' sake if we sincerely repent and follow Jesus.

Making a choice

Life offers many choices, but eternity offers only two: heaven or hell. Which are you going to choose? You can choose the immediate gratification of worldly pleasures and gains, or you can choose the eternal joy of living forever with Jesus and fellow believers in his kingdom. The Bible is clear that the least significant thing in heaven is more wonderful and glorious than the most splendid thing on earth.

If you say you're a Christian but live as if you don't know Jesus, you have chosen the world. If you attend church but don't obey God's commands, you have chosen the world. If you talk about Jesus but don't obey God, you have chosen the world. Those who choose the world over God, whether they call themselves Christians or not, choose hell.

> Therefore, put to death whatever is worldly in you: your sexual sin, perversion, passion, lust, and greed (which is the same thing as worshiping wealth). It is because of these sins that God's anger comes on those who refuse to obey him. You used to live that kind of sinful life. Also get rid of your anger, hot tempers, hatred, cursing, obscene language, and all similar sins. Don't lie to each other. You've gotten rid of the person you used to be and the life you used to live, and you've become a new person. This new person is continually renewed in knowledge to be like its Creator. (Col. 3:5–10)

Many Christians believe they would lay down their life for Christ if placed in a situation where they must deny Jesus or be killed. But if you aren't laying down your life for Christ on a daily basis by listening to the Holy Spirit and being obedient to God's will for your life, it's highly unlikely you would stand up for Christ in the face of threatened loss of job, home, family, or even life. You think you would. You believe you would, but if you aren't picking up your cross every day and following Jesus, chances are you'll deny him when faced with loss, injury, or death. Disobedient Christians really don't know Jesus at all.

If in your heart you know you need to and are ready to repent of being a disobedient Christian, you can say this prayer.

Dear Father, please forgive me for not obeying your commandments and your will for my life. My life is a mess because it doesn't really include you and what you want for me. My life has been all about me. Please urge me by your Holy Spirit to overcome temptation and obey you in all areas of my life, including giving my tithes and offerings as you direct. I accept Jesus as my Lord and Savior and look forward to the day when he will return to take me and all believers to heaven to live with you forever in your glorious kingdom. In Jesus' name I pray. Amen.

4

The Drunkards

I've told you in the past and I'm telling you again that people who do things like that will not inherit the kingdom of God. (Gal. 5:21)

*Sheila is a binge drinker. She may go several weeks without a drink, but once she starts drinking, she won't stop until she has passed out. *Larry is a daily drinker. Since he retired, he enjoys going to the corner bar and drinking with his buddies all day. By the time he returns home for dinner, he's intoxicated. *Pete is a social drinker. Bored with his life, he goes to the bar to shoot darts and drink with his friends. Although he tries not to get drunk, Pete usually ends up exceeding his limit and going home intoxicated. *Betty likes to drink at home. Her days begin and end with a scotch on the rocks. Edward was a mail carrier. He'd be sure to stop at the bar before ending his shift. His excuse was that mail carriers were not allowed back into the postal station until 4 p.m. He often finished by 2 p.m. and was always way over the limit when his shift ended.

Drunkards hurt everyone

The Bible tells us drunkards will not inherit the kingdom of heaven. Notice it doesn't say, "those who drink." It clearly says *drunkards*. So, why drunks, anyway? What has God got against a harmless drunk? How is he hurting anyone but himself?

If you're living with an alcoholic or drug addict in your life, you are well aware of how he hurts himself and everyone around him with his drinking. His job, finances, and health suffer, along with all his relationships. He starts lying and stops being dependable. Clouded by the drugs or alcohol, the addicted person's mind is open to every confusion and deception of the devil.

> Don't you know that you are God's temple and that God's Spirit lives in you? If anyone destroys God's temple, God will destroy him because God's temple is holy. You are that holy temple! (1 Cor. 3:16–17)

The drunkard or drug addict will spend his very last dollar on a drink or drugs to keep the drunk or stoned feeling going. When he needs a drink, it doesn't matter if there isn't any food in the house, if the kids need clothes, if there are bills to pay. Selfish ambitions take over, and no one or nothing matters but the next fix. Alcoholics and drug addicts care about no one but themselves. The Bible tells us not to even associate with someone who overindulges in alcohol.

> Do not associate with those who drink too much wine, with those who eat too much meat, because both a drunk and a glutton will become poor. Drowsiness will dress a person in rags. (Prov. 23:20–21)

My husband worked with a fireman who became addicted to both drugs and alcohol. *Barry's drinking and drugging cost him his job, then his home, then his friends and family. He is now homeless and living under a viaduct a half mile from our house. Friends and family who have taken him in and tried to help him have found that he is also a thief. Yes, alcoholics and drug addicts will steal from anyone when the money is gone and the body cries out for the next fix.

Barry started drinking shortly after high school when he enlisted in the military, and now, twenty years later, he has not been able to kick the habit. He added drugs to the mix a few years after being discharged from the service and is still addicted to crack cocaine. Many young people today probably started out much the same as Barry, with a few drinks or a joint here or there, which quickly escalated from "I want this," to "I need this," to "I've got to have this no matter what it costs me."

College campuses are swarming with students who live to party and drink. Getting drunk has even become a popular initiation or hazing for students wanting to get into select groups or clubs. Several students have died while binge drinking in their attempts to join a fraternity or sorority.

Some on the city council of La Crosse, Wisconsin, want to fence off the Mississippi River near the downtown taverns because, almost without fail, drunken students are diving into the river and drowning. Nothing good can come from alcohol or drugs, which is why the Bible warns people to stay away from them.

> We should live decently, as people who live in the light of day. Wild parties, drunkenness, sexual immorality, promiscuity, rivalry, and jealousy cannot be

part of our lives. Instead, live like the Lord Jesus Christ did, and forget about satisfying the desires of your sinful nature. (Rom. 13:13–14)

Don't get drunk on wine, which leads to wild living. Instead, be filled with the Spirit. (Eph 5:18)

Drugs and alcohol destroy the body as well as the mind and soul. Alcohol causes blood vessels to burst, especially on the face and nose. It is responsible for liver and kidney failure and destroys brain cells. It all but kills developing fetuses. God wants us to keep our bodies pure and our minds focused on him. This can't happen when we seek to gratify our flesh or numb our pain by drinking or drugging. God wants us to find peace, joy, comfort, and our destiny in him. Anything we turn to other than him for these things is an idol. As we intentionally drink and drug to numb our minds and we voluntarily give up self–control, which is a gift of the Holy Spirit, we open ourselves up to all kinds of demonic activity, which quickly takes a stronghold that can be broken only by the power of Jesus' blood.

Don't you know that your body is a temple that belongs to the Holy Spirit? The Holy Spirit, whom you received from God, lives in you. You don't belong to yourselves. You were bought for a price. So bring glory to God in the way you use your body. (1 Cor. 6:19–20)

A way out

Jesus came to destroy the works of the devil and to set the captives free by breaking the power of sin and death. One of the benefits of the Great Exchange is receiving deliverance from every bondage to sin. Call out to Jesus to deliver you from addiction; he will be faithful to answer you.

We curse the alcoholic by telling him, "Once an alcoholic, always an alcoholic." Jesus has the power to set you completely free. He doesn't want to turn you into a recovering addict; he wants to turn you into a non–addict. Sometimes he does this quickly, sometimes over time, but he has promised to do it.

The Lord sets prisoners free. (Ps. 146:7)

Some alcoholics and addicts have found help through the twelve steps of Alcoholics Anonymous. In Step One, the alcoholic admits he is powerless over alcohol, that his life has become unmanageable. Let's change a couple of words. Step

One: I am powerless over sin, and my life has become unmanageable. Step Two: I believe God can restore me to sanity. Step Three: I turn my will and my life over to the Lord Jesus Christ and accept his atonement for my sin. I put my faith in his blood that cleanses me continually and in his Holy Spirit, who works in me with resurrection power. You can put down the bottle of booze and drink of the water of life instead, and you'll never be thirsty again.

> It is God who produces in you the desires and actions that please him. (Philippians 2:13)
>
> Freed from sin, you were made slaves who do what God approves of. (Rom. 6:18)
>
> Let those who are thirsty come! Let those who want the water of life take it as a gift. (Rev. 22:17)
>
> But those who drink the water that I will give them will never become thirsty again. In fact, the water I will give them will become in them a spring that gushes up to eternal life. (John 4:14)

An actor was arrested in Los Angeles County for driving while legally drunk. During his arrest, he made derogatory remarks about God's chosen people, the Jews. There are those who will say this man was expressing his true feelings about the Jews because he was drunk. He claims the obscenities he spoke and the anti–Semitic remarks were caused by the alcohol, that they don't represent his true feelings about Jewish people.[1]

The most likely scenario is that Satan, who hates God's chosen people, the Jews, found the actor's weakness, alcohol, and continually tempted him with it. Knowing that this man has brought many people to Jesus through his films and through his witnessing, the devil wanted to bring the actor down. It's a lot easier for Satan to control a person who is inebriated. The man fell into Satan's hands and was used as a pawn to espouse evil.

Thankfully, he immediately repented of his words and actions, expressed remorse, and asked those whom he had harmed to forgive him.[2] The sin, although not readily forgotten by the public, is completely erased from God's memory thanks to Jesus' death on the cross in our place.

Is alcoholism a disease?

We're told that alcoholism is a disease, but is it really? At one time alcoholism was considered to be bondage to sin, and it still is to God. Alcoholics Anonymous refers to alcoholism as an "illness." So which one is it? Is abusing alcohol an illness or is it sin? It's the only "illness" that can result in fines, jail time, loss of a driver's license, or result in your children being removed from your home by social services. It's the only "illness" that can cause you to do things you later wish you hadn't done.

Let's look at how the "illness" of alcoholism is diagnosed. AA literature tells us only the alcoholic can determine if he or she is an alcoholic. Huh? How many other illnesses are diagnosed in this manner? None that I can think of. Can you imagine a doctor telling a patient that only the patient can determine whether or not he has heart disease, lung disease, cancer, or any other diseases? It's nonsense. Stop kidding yourself. Alcoholism is a disease all right; it's the disease of sin! The good news is that there's a cure: the Great Exchange, exchanging your life for Christ's life in you.

For unrepentant drunks and addicts, the alcohol or drug is their god. They have not believed on the name of the Lord Jesus Christ to set them free from bondage to this sin. God says you are to have no other gods but him. When discussing the First Commandment, Martin Luther said: "That upon which you place your trust is, in reality, your god."

You must choose between your addiction and God. I'm not saying to stop attending your AA meetings if you find them helpful. I'm saying that regardless of whether you view your addiction as a disease or as sin, God can and will deliver you from alcoholism or drug addiction. Jesus has already done the hard work for you, all you have to do is accept it and make that Great Exchange.

If in your heart you know you need to and are ready to repent of being in bondage to alcohol or drugs, please pray this prayer.

Dear Father, please forgive me for not respecting my body as a temple of the Holy Spirit. I am sorry for all the times I have abused my body with alcohol and/or drugs. Forgive me for all the people I've hurt with my behavior and bless and keep them. Show me how to make amends. I accept Jesus' sacrifice on the cross as the atonement for all the times I've gotten drunk or stoned and for all my sins. Please change my heart so that I will live for you, free from any bondage to sin. Help me to call on you when I'm tempted to drink or do drugs. I accept you, Jesus, as my Lord and Savior and look forward to the day when you'll return to take me and other believers to heaven to live with you forever in your glorious kingdom. In Jesus' name I pray. Amen.

5

The Envious, Jealous and Covetous

A tranquil heart makes for a healthy body, but jealousy is like bone cancer. (Prov. 14:30)

Seeing his neighbor's new car made *Frank unhappy. Envy got the best of him, and he traded in his older model car for one that was just a little bit nicer than the neighbor's. Frank can barely make ends meet trying to make payments on the new vehicle.

*Laura was jealous that her friend's recently published book was doing well in sales because Laura had been trying in vain for two years to publish her own book. Jealousy and hatefulness took over, and Laura began doing everything she could think of to sabotage her friend's book sales.

*Scott coveted his best friend's wife to the point that he wanted his friend dead. Covetousness and thoughts of murder ruled his decision to hire someone to kill his best friend.

Precursor to worse sins

Jealousy, envy, and covetousness lead to all kinds of deadly sins, including, but not limited to, adultery, greed, theft, and murder. Vandalism is most often the result of envy or jealousy. God tells us we should be content with what we have. He felt so strongly about these sins that he included them in his Ten Commandments and promised eternal damnation for covetousness.

> Never desire to take your neighbor's household away from him. Never desire to take your neighbor's wife, his male or female slave, his ox, his donkey, or anything else that belongs to him. (Ex. 20:17)

Envy wants what someone else has. Jealousy resents that they have it. Covetousness seeks a way to get it and make it yours. Envy and jealousy are sins of the heart. Coveting starts in the heart and leads to action, which is why it is a commandment along with the other "shall nots." Jesus might have said, "Whoever envies another man his good fortune has already committed coveting in his heart."

Just so we're clear, not all coveting is wrong. You may covet a college education. That isn't sinful coveting. To covet something that you can obtain by legal, ethical, or moral means is not the kind of coveting God forbids.

Cain killed his brother Abel because he was jealous of Abel's relationship with God. David had Uriah, the Hittite and husband of Bathsheba, killed because David had coveted Bathsheba. Jacob coveted his brother Esau's birthright of the double portion of Isaac's estate as the firstborn son, and he induced his brother to sell it to him. These acts come from hearts focused on self, not on love. Jealousy, envy, and coveting inevitably lead to acts of hate.

> Love is patient. Love is kind. Love isn't jealous. It doesn't sing its own praises. It isn't arrogant.(1 Cor. 13:4)

The evil thoughts that go through our heads when we're envious of another are not pleasing to God. When we're jealous of someone's position at work, when we envy our neighbor's new car, when we covet someone else's spouse, Satan is at work putting greedy, adulterous, murderous, and other evil thoughts in our minds.

> Wherever there is jealousy and rivalry, there is disorder and every kind of evil. (James 3:16)

A young woman, just eighteen years old, visited four young men in their home and coveted their block of queso fresco (cheese), which she mistook for cocaine. Selfish ambitions entered her mind, and she decided if only she could possess the "cocaine," she could sell it to pay for modeling school. These selfish ambitions led to thoughts of murder, and she hired an undercover police officer posing as a hit man to murder the four men and any witnesses who might be present.[1]

In this case, the sin of coveting had led to the sin of having selfish ambitions, which had led to the sin of having murder in her heart. Coveting someone else's property led this young woman down a dark path where she was willing to sacrifice the lives of several others to get what she wanted.

Sinful coveting takes place in the sinful heart. The temptation to covet is not sinful in itself. Coveting is sinful when one's mind begins to plot a way to obtain that which cannot legally, ethically, or morally be obtained. In other words, when the thing desired requires the breaking of any other commandment to obtain, it is sinful coveting.

Controlled by our sinful selves

We should be happy for our neighbor's or co-worker's good fortune and pray for God to continue to bless them. When we focus our thoughts on the well-being of the other person, rather than on ourselves, jealous thoughts won't surface.

> You're still influenced by your corrupt nature. When you are jealous and quarrel among yourselves, aren't you influenced by your corrupt nature and living by human standards? (1 Cor. 3:3)

When we're thinking about possessions and ambitions, we may not be thinking about God. God knows our wants and needs and will provide for us on his own timing. When we thank and praise him daily for that which he has already blessed us, when we show true contentment with what we have, then we get our minds off Satan's agenda and attempts to fill our hearts with envy and jealousy. It is right to plan for our futures, even what we choose as our calling in life. However, everything in our plans must be according to God's will and purpose for our lives.

> What causes fights and quarrels among you? Aren't they caused by the selfish desires that fight to control you? You want what you don't have, so you commit murder. You're determined to have things, but you can't get what you want. You quarrel and fight. You don't have the things you want because you don't pray for them. When you pray for things, you don't get them because you want them for the wrong reason—for your own pleasure. (James 4:1–3)

Jealousy, envy, and covetousness are signs that we are being controlled by our sinful selves, rather than turning our will and our life over to God through the Great Exchange. It is a sign to God that we don't love and trust him above all things, which is why these cherished sins are so spiritually lethal they eventually lead to hell.

> Those who live by the corrupt nature have the corrupt nature's attitude. But those who live by the spiritual nature have the spiritual nature's attitude. The corrupt nature's attitude leads to death. But the spiritual nature's attitude leads to life and peace. This is so because the corrupt nature has a hostile attitude toward God. It refuses to place itself under the authority of God's standards because it can't. Those who are under the control of the corrupt nature can't please God. (Rom. 8:5–8)

Envy, jealousy, and coveting are often the result of sinful pride operating in our lives. When we can replace pride with humbleness and humility, then envy, jealousy, and coveting will disappear. We need to realize that everything we are and everything we have, especially our talents and possessions, are because of God's grace and mercy. We are even called to defend and protect those of our neighbor as well. Pride causes us to want to be better than other people, to have more or to be able to do more, to want our children to surpass our neighbors' children in academic or athletic success. Pride causes us to become envious or jealous of our neighbor. When we can accept the fact that we are nothing and God is everything, only then can we begin to develop some humility.

However, we must remember that it is not wrong to have ambition. In fact it is right to use the gifts, intelligence, and strengths we've been given by God to bring him a return on the investment he made in us. It is not sinful pride to have ambition. Ambition alone is proper, but, just like coveting, if it takes the breaking of any other commandment to achieve our goal, ambition has been corrupted by pride. When Jesus told the parable of the talents, he let us know that God expects good stewardship of the gifts he has given to us. (Matt. 25:15)

> Who says that you are any better than other people? What do you have that wasn't given to you? If you were given what you have, why are you bragging as if it weren't a gift? (1 Cor. 4:7)

Practicing humility requires us to truly love our neighbor as ourself. It may even require us to put the other person's wants, needs, feelings, and opinions ahead of our own. Parents do this as a matter of second nature for their children. It requires us to speak humbly and modestly about ourselves and our accomplishments. It requires us to put God first, others next, and ourselves last. Humility is the key to ridding ourselves of the damning sin of covetousness.

> Those who honor themselves will be humbled, but people who humble themselves will be honored. (Luke 14:11)

If in your heart you know you need to and are ready to repent of envy, jealousy, and covetousness, please pray this prayer.

Dear Father, please forgive me for my sins of envy, jealousy, and covetousness. Help me to be content with what I have and not to desire or try to take things that others have. Teach me to rejoice when others are blessed and to expect good things to come to me directly from you. I accept Jesus as my Lord and Savior and know I am cleansed of these sins and all my sins by his death on the cross and his resurrection. I look forward to the day when Jesus will return to take me and all believers to heaven to live with you forever in your glorious kingdom. In Jesus' name I pray. Amen.

6

The Greedy

Be careful to guard yourselves from every kind of greed. Life is not about having a lot of material possessions. (Luke: 12:15)

The theme song to the television reality show *The Apprentice* begins, "Money, money, money, money." Contestants vie for a $250,000 per year salaried position with a real estate investment organization. Those who have mastered the show's greed ethic usually make it to the final round. Neither consideration for others nor ethics are considered admirable traits in contestants. In one episode, a female contestant refused to wear a silly costume for fear she would embarrass her family and employers, who were from a conservative culture in another country. She was fired for not being a team player. In another episode, two contestants "stole" megaphones the other team had reserved for themselves at a local Radio Shack. They were lauded by the CEO for their ingenuity, rather than chastised for taking something that belonged to someone else.

This CEO's real estate investments have made him a multi–millionaire, but he won't be taking any buildings or money with him when he dies. He would be wise to invest in his eternal home, to store up treasures that will last forever.

Precursor to worse sins

Television commercials, magazine articles, and billboards plaster the messages all over: You need more stuff. You need better stuff. You need our stuff. If you buy this car, the women will swarm all over you. If you buy this toy for your child, she will love you. If you don't buy these expensive fancy jeans, you can't hang with the in crowd. They turn your wants into needs until they've convinced you that you *have* to have their things.

> A godly life brings huge profits to people who are content with what they have. We didn't bring anything into the world, and we can't take anything out

of it. As long as we have food and clothes, we should be satisfied. (1 Tim. 6:6–8)

Greedy people want lots of money, power, control, and things, and many will stop at nothing to satisfy their greed. A greedy man brings trouble to his family and to himself.

> This is what happens to everyone who is greedy for unjust gain. Greed takes away his life. (Prov. 1:19)

A woman bought herself three thousand pairs of shoes while children ran barefoot in the streets outside her door.[1] Enron executives bankrupted their employees and shareholders in their greed for wealth.[2] A Milwaukee church bookkeeper embezzled $518,659 from church collections over two years to feed a gambling habit.[3] A Pittsburgh priest embezzled $1.5 million over 25 years to purchase fancy cars, antique guns, and to support his gambling addiction.[4]

> Certainly, the love of money is the root of all kinds of evil. Some people who have set their hearts on getting rich have wandered away from the Christian faith and have caused themselves a lot of grief. (1 Tim. 6:10)

Robberies, burglaries, extortion, murder—most are fueled by greed. People commit these crimes in the hopes of improving their situations, increasing their wealth, and gaining possessions (or to keep from losing them).

> Do not wear yourself out getting rich. Be smart enough to stop. (Prov. 23:4)

If you Google "lottery winners two years later," you will find headline after headline declaring things like "lost their money," "squabbles with relatives," "lottery win brings heartache." Many people who have made it to the top of their professions and have won all the fame, money, and acclaim there is, have testified that these things did not make them happy. Money doesn't satisfy the heart.

> Whoever loves money will never be satisfied with money. Whoever loves wealth will never be satisfied with more income. Even this is pointless. (Ecc. 5:10)

Gluttony is a form of greed too. God gave us food for nourishment and enjoyment, but it is displeasing to him when we overindulge ourselves. He wants us to trust him to provide for us on a daily basis. When God provided manna to the Israelites daily for 40 years, he told them to take only what they needed for that day, not to store the extra manna but to leave it on the ground. In the same manner, he wants us to eat what we need to nourish our bodies and to discard the extra. He knows it isn't healthy for our bodies when we overindulge on food, and he's angered by our lack of trust in him to supply all the food we need each day. He knew how we humans would worry about tomorrow. A better translation of a part of the Lord's Prayer is this: "Give us today *tomorrow's* bread. God knew we'd worry, so he teaches us to pray with the future of our needs in his hands.

> When you sit down to eat with a ruler, pay close attention to what is in front of you, and put a knife to your throat if you have a big appetite. Do not crave his delicacies, because this is food that deceives you. (Prov. 23:1–3)

> Do not associate with those who drink too much wine, with those who eat too much meat, because both a drunk and a glutton will become poor. Drowsiness will dress a person in rags. (Prov. 23:20–21)

Greed and the rich man

Jesus tells us it will be difficult for a rich man to enter heaven. This is because accepting Jesus as our Lord and Savior requires us to stop focusing on ourselves. We are to put God first and others next, trusting God to take care of us. That's a hard thing to do when you have a lot more money and possessions than the next guy.

> Jesus said to his disciples, "I can guarantee this truth: It will be hard for a rich person to enter the kingdom of heaven. I can guarantee again that it is easier for a camel to go through the eye of a needle than for a rich person to enter the kingdom of God. (Matt. 19:23–24)

Jesus says it is hard for a rich person to enter heaven, but he doesn't say it is impossible. He tells how it can be accomplished.

> Jesus said to him, "If you want to be perfect, sell what you own. Give the money to the poor, and you will have treasure in heaven. Then follow me!" (Matt. 19:21)

Does Jesus literally want us to go and sell everything we have? He wants us to be willing to if he asks it of us; if we trust him to take care of us, we will be willing. He asks this of some and not of others. The point is this: God wants us to have peaceful and joy-filled lives. He knows this only happens when we keep our focus on and our trust in him.

If God wants us to give up homes and cars, he will reveal this to us and will give us the peace and strength to do it. He always wants us to be content with what we have and to be willing to share with others. When we follow Jesus, we may have seasons of plenty and seasons of not having very much, but we won't mind because, once we've made the Great Exchange, Christ will give us the strength to endure any hardships.

> I've learned to be content in whatever situation I'm in. I know how to live in poverty or prosperity. No matter what the situation, I've learned the secret of how to live when I'm full or when I'm hungry, when I have too much or when I have too little. I can do everything through Christ who strengthens me. (Phil. 4:11–13)

*Dr. Ken Webster, a Presbyterian dentist who professes to be a Christian, opened his dental practice about twenty-five years ago. He wasn't originally motivated by greed. He desired to provide dental care to all who needed it, rich and poor alike. In the early years of his practice, he accepted Medicaid, often lowered his fees for those without insurance, made house calls to elderly and disabled patients, and would even send an employee to give a ride to the patient who lived nearby but wasn't able to obtain transportation.

God was pleased with Dr. Webster's servitude and blessed him in all areas of his personal and business life. His practice grew from one dental assistant and receptionist to two dental assistants, two receptionists, three hygienists, and an associate dentist.

Dr. Webster wasn't content with the success of his practice and financial blessings. Having experienced a taste of the rich life, he wanted more. He was no longer satisfied with sending his children to a $10,000 per year private school but longed to enroll them in the $20,000 per year school. He stopped accepting Medicaid because there was no profit in it. He no longer lowered his fees for the poor. If a patient didn't have insurance and couldn't afford his fees, they would just have to go elsewhere. He stopped making house calls to the elderly and disabled because it cut into his money-making time. No longer did he send an employee to pick up a patient who needed a ride. Whatever amount a patient's insurance wouldn't cover, he insisted on receiving at the time of the appointment, even if it was just a few dollars, rather than waiting for the insurance company to pay and then billing the patient.

Dr. Webster raised his fees considerably each year. Not one year went by during those twenty-five years when he kept fees the same or lowered them. He did share profits with his employees, but it was on an incentive basis. The more money they made for him, the more they received back. He packed up his wife and kids and moved to an affluent neighborhood where he is now living "the good life."

But is it good? Greed took Dr. Webster away from his core Christian beliefs and set him on the path of destruction. Money became the all-important motivating factor, and he was willing to empty his patients' pocketbooks so that he and his family could live a life of luxury. Come judgment day, God may not even recognize Dr. Webster as belonging to him.

> Rich believers should be proud because being rich should make them humble. Rich people wither like flowers. The sun rises with its scorching heat and dries up plants. The flowers drop off, and the beauty is gone. The same thing will happen to rich people. While they are busy, they will die. (James 1:10–11)

Frivolous lawsuits

Those who file frivolous lawsuits could be written about in a number of chapters of this book, including the chapter on thieves and the chapter on those who have selfish ambitions. However, the underlying motive of those who file ridiculous lawsuits is to better their financial situation at the expense of others—in other words, the greedy.

A lawsuit against McDonald's is probably the most well-known case that caused mouths to drop open when an elderly woman actually won in court. She had sued McDonald's because its coffee was too hot. Apparently, she spilled some of the coffee in her lap and received some burns, sued the fast-food restaurant, and was awarded $2.9 million dollars. The amount was later reduced to $650,000.[5]

Parents sued a taco chain because their child was burned by some nacho cheese which was too hot. A hunter sued an ammunition manufacturer for failing to place a label on the ammunition to warn purchasers that the ammo isn't suitable for killing a charging lion. Parents are suing fast food chains because their children are obese. I was in a jury pool (but not selected) to hear a case about a man who had walked through a glass window at a car dealership. He filed suit because the windows were too clean for him to be able to see there was glass present.

We must be responsible for our own actions and, yes, for our own stupidity. Every time something bad happens or we get injured doesn't mean someone else is to blame. Whether we, as Christians, are the victims of a mishap, whether we are the lawyers or the jurors, we need to look at every situation as Jesus would. The lawyers who are filing these lawsuits need to repent, the jurors who are awarding money to victims of their own stupidity need to repent, and the victims who are filing these lawsuits need to repent of being greedy or assisting others in their greed. We shouldn't participate in frivolous class action suits that award victims a few dollars, that award attorneys hundreds of thousands of dollars, and that bankrupt businesses.

Some people even go so far in their greed as to sue a family member, friend, neighbor, or their own church for perceived injuries or slights. Jesus tells us in Matthew 18 the four steps Christians should follow in their disputes with other believers. Nowhere in those steps does it say to take the other person to court and attempt to bankrupt him or her for your injury. I'm sure God's not happy someone would sue for a couple million dollars over spilled coffee or hot nachos.

> If a believer does something wrong, go confront him when the two of you are alone. If he listens to you, you have won back that believer. But if he does not listen, take one or two others with you so that every accusation may be verified by two or three witnesses. If he ignores these witnesses, tell it to the community of believers. If he also ignores the community, deal with him as you would a heathen or a tax collector. (Matt. 18:15–18)

Giving back to God

Those who aren't greedy give God his fair share and beyond. God expects us to first give back to him with our tithe (10 percent), which he says belongs to him.

> "Can a person cheat God? Yet, you are cheating me! But you ask, 'How are we cheating you?' When you don't bring a tenth of your income and other contributions. So a curse is on you because the whole nation is cheating me. Bring one–tenth of your income into the storehouse so that there may be food in my house. Test me in this way," says the Lord of Armies. "See if I won't open the windows of heaven for you and flood you with blessings." (Mal. 3:8–10)

When we tithe, we aren't *giving* God 10 percent; he's allowing us to *keep* 90 percent. God will bless that 90 percent to cover more than we could imagine when we're not greedy. To serve God wholeheartedly, we must tithe.

> No one can serve two masters. He will hate the first master and love the second, or he will be devoted to the first and despise the second. You cannot serve God and wealth. (Matt: 6:24)

What's the point of accumulating a lot of things, even if they are nice things? You can't take any of your things with you when you die. I have never seen a U-Haul following a hearse.

> Do you not know that wicked people won't inherit the kingdom of God? Stop deceiving yourselves! Those who are greedy will not inherit the kingdom of God. (1 Cor. 6:10)

> Jesus said, "Stop storing up treasures for yourselves on earth, where moths and rust destroy and thieves break in and steal. Instead, store up treasures for yourselves in heaven, where moths and rust don't destroy and thieves don't break in and steal. Your heart will be where your treasure is." (Matt. 6:19–21)

If in your heart you know you need to and are ready to repent of being greedy, please pray this prayer.

Dear Father, please forgive me for being greedy. Forgive me for loving money and possessions more than you. From this moment on may I consider everything I have as belonging to you. Help me to be generous and obedient with what you have blessed me with that I might give more to you and to those in need. I accept Jesus as my Lord and Savior and look forward to the day when he will return to take me and all believers to heaven to live with you forever in your glorious kingdom. In Jesus' name I pray. Amen.

7

The Hateful

You have heard that it was said, 'Love your neighbor and hate your enemy.' But I tell you this: Love your enemies and pray for those who persecute you that you are children of your Father in heaven. (Matt. 5:43–44)

When *Marie's father died, no one from her husband's family attended the wake or funeral—not her mother- or father-in-law, not her sister- or brother-in law, not her niece or nephew. Marie asked her sister-in-law, *Leah, why none had come, and Leah said, "We didn't know your father that well."

Most people are aware that funerals are for the living, not the dead. After a little more prodding, Leah told Marie, "We didn't come to your dad's funeral because we were mad at you for driving *Dean [Leah's husband and a recovering alcoholic] to a bar last month."

Leah learned several weeks after the funeral that it was Dean who had driven Marie (also a recovering alcoholic) to the bar, but instead of apologizing to Marie and asking for forgiveness for her hateful act of carrying a grudge for a month and boycotting the funeral, Leah chose to gloat in the glory of having hurt someone in such a spiteful, calculated way. Marie's husband's family held on to their anger and hatred so long that when Marie's mother died a few years later, none in her husband's family attended that funeral either.

One of Marie's friends suggested to her that perhaps Marie should boycott the next funeral in her husband's family. Marie replied, "I could never be that hateful. I will attend the funerals in my husband's family and will invite my other family members to attend as well. I'm going to return hatefulness with kindness and forgive my in-laws for their hatefulness." That's exactly what she did. When her father-in-law's sister died, Marie attended the funeral and was able to associate with all as if the hateful act towards her had never occurred. True forgiveness always means removing the offense from your mind and continuing the relationship as if the offense had never occurred.

Those who hate, who cause discord, dissensions, or factions, or who have fits of rage will not inherit the kingdom of heaven. We have all met a hateful person. He is the guy at work who always keeps things stirred up. She is the neighbor who is forever quarreling with other neighbors about petty things. It is the man who throws a fit every time a kid steps on his lawn. It is the lady at church who is constantly complaining about something or criticizing someone. It is the gossiper, the arguer, the opinionated person who is always right, the classroom snitch, the angry driver ... the list goes on and on.

Fits of rage

We all get angry sometimes. Getting angry is not necessarily sinful, depending on what you're angry about, but the Bible says when we get angry, we should not sin in our anger.

Jesus became angry when merchants had turned God's house into a marketplace, making it about profit instead of worship. On three separate occasions when he was in Jerusalem, Jesus overturned the tables and benches of those who were selling items in the church because they were cheating his people. His anger was righteous anger. Christians show righteous anger when they see the oppressed being ignored and the poor not being cared for. They show righteous anger in the face of attempts by judges and legislators to ban freedom of religious speech from the public square. They may also have righteous anger at other's attempts to legalize things the Bible says are sinful.

Is anger mostly righteous anger? I doubt it. Some people burst into fits of rage and display violent tempers when the smallest thing goes wrong or doesn't go their way. The Bible has a lot to say about this person.

> A person of great understanding is patient, but a short temper is the height of stupidity. (Prov. 14:29)
>
> A fool expresses all his emotions, but a wise person controls them. (Prov. 29:11)

Three young men, in their prejudice and rage, chained James Bird to the back of their pickup truck and dragged him through the streets until there was nothing left of him but a bloody, mangled corpse. One of the men said later he knew Mr. Bird and really didn't want to go along with the plans of the others. He felt he was trapped, that if he didn't participate, they might do the same things to him they had planned for Mr. Bird.[1] He had fallen into the trap the Bible warns us about which comes to those who befriend people filled with anger.

> Do not be a friend of one who has a bad temper, and never keep company with a hothead, or you will learn his ways and set a trap for yourself. (Prov. 22:24–25)

A woman, in a fit of rage, killed a grandmother in a dispute over a parking space. She pulled the older woman to the ground and repeatedly kicked her in the face, causing the grandmother's death.[2] This woman is an example of what happens when we let anger control us. She was willing to take the life of another person to gain a prime parking spot!

Quite often when we become angry, we have already sinned in our thoughts. We have placed our own agenda ahead of everyone else's. We have considered that what we want is more important than what anyone else wants, and we are at that moment being tempted to sin in our words and deeds. If we don't check the self-focused, angry thoughts, we may speak angry words or profanity; some people even explode in violent acts of rage. Or, we may seethe silently for a long time, which medical science has shown will make us ill. Rather than immediately getting angry in a given situation, God expects us to keep our peace and quickly forgive whomever we need to forgive, just as he is slow to become angry with us but is always quick to forgive our sins.

> Remember this, my dear brothers and sisters: Everyone should be quick to listen, slow to speak, and should not get angry easily. An angry person doesn't do what God approves of. So get rid of all immoral behavior and all the wicked things you do. Humbly accept the word that God has placed in you. This word can save you. (James 1:19–21)

Road rage

Road rage has become a common occurrence on the streets and highways throughout America. A young man became so enraged at a woman who had bumped into him in traffic that he stripped her clothes off and pummeled her with a tire iron for ten minutes, causing her to jump off a bridge to her death in an effort to get away from him.[3]

A driver, in a fit of rage, tossed another driver's small dog into traffic when she bumped into him in traffic. He was sentenced to three years in jail for the crime.[4]

These unremorseful, unrepentant, angry people haven't made the Great Exchange, and unless they do, their chances of seeing heaven are slim.

Rage must be replaced with a humble heart and humility. We must put other drivers and other people above ourselves, loving them as Christ loves us. When we're seething with rage over some real or imagined slight, we are as far from God as we can possibly be. It isn't Christ who is living in us, but Satan. Once upon a time we were taught to count to ten, slowly, and let stupid things and real or imagined hurts pass. When did parents stop teaching that to their children?

> Get rid of your bitterness, hot tempers, anger, loud quarreling, cursing, and hatred. Be kind to each other, sympathetic, forgiving each other as God has forgiven you through Christ. (Eph. 4:31–32)

Discordant, contentious, creating factions

The person who is always trying to stir up trouble, to start fights and disagreements, to cause brother to turn against brother, co-worker to turn against co-worker, neighbor to turn against neighbor, will not inherit the kingdom of heaven.

> Now, the effects of the corrupt nature are obvious: ... hatred, rivalry, ... angry outbursts, selfish ambition, conflict, factions ... and things like that. I've told you in the past and I'm telling you again that people who do things like that will not inherit the kingdom of God. (Gal. 5:19–21)

A clothing company based in Florida created a line of "Boys are Stupid" t-shirts which they market to adolescent girls. The shirts have slogans such as, "Boys are stupid; throw rocks at them," and portray a picture of a boy running away with rocks sailing at his head. The company insists the shirts are intended to be funny.[5]

Insults and name calling are never funny. They are hateful, hurtful, and harmful, and set one group against another. God despises this kind of attitude and behavior; he wants us to be loving, kind, and respectful to others. He wants us to love and forgive each other and to avoid strife and disharmony.

> Hate starts quarrels, but love covers every wrong. (Prov:10:12)

> Wherever there is jealousy and rivalry, there is disorder and every kind of evil. (James 3:16)

It's okay to disagree with someone, but we need to do it peaceably and without holding anything against them. Gossiping, name calling, bringing up past wrongs, making the disagreement personal—these are not ways God wants his people to handle conflicts. He expects us to love each person he sends our way and to treat them with dignity and respect, whether we agree with them or not. Dissension is not Godly. Satan is always at work trying to create discord and factions because he knows it leads to our destruction.

> A good–for–nothing scoundrel is a person who has a dishonest mouth. He winks his eye, makes a signal with his foot, and points with his fingers. He devises evil all the time with a twisted mind. He spreads conflict. That is why disaster will come on him suddenly. In a moment he will be crushed beyond recovery. (Prov. 6:12–15)

A woman who worked in a dental office was constantly whining and complaining and keeping everyone and everything in the office in turmoil. She frequently gossiped and would try to get everyone upset when appointments were running behind schedule or when it looked as though she would have to work through her lunch hour or after hours. She even complained when she didn't receive her bonus (a generous gift from the dentist each month) at the expected time! It was a very stressful work environment for all who worked with her. When she left to take another job, all discord and dissension among employees stopped. Satan had been using one person to try to bring down the entire office staff.

> A devious person spreads quarrels. A gossip separates the closest of friends. (Prov. 16:28)

Hatred

If we attend church regularly, give everything we have to the poor, and know the Bible from cover to cover, but we don't love our neighbor, we won't inherit the kingdom of heaven. God alone knows those who call themselves Christians and show their Sunday piety, yet on Monday morning they are steaming with hate.

A woman wrote and published a very insightful Christian book about how one political party is working with the ACLU to harass Christians through an overabundance of lawsuits. The book was well written and contained a plethora of information. The author, however, resorted to name calling, and her hatred for the ACLU and the political party came across on almost every page. Although she had attempted to stand up for Christians and for Jesus, the book wasn't written in a spirit of love, so the message was lost amid the hate.

> I may speak in the languages of humans and of angels. But if I don't have love, I am a loud gong or a clashing cymbal. I may have the gift to speak what God has revealed, and I may understand all mysteries and have all knowledge. I may even have enough faith to move mountains. But if I don't have love, I am nothing. I may even give away all that I have and give up my body to be burned. But if I don't have love, none of these things will help me. (1Cor. 13:1–3)

Love is not warm, fuzzy feelings, although if we love persistently, these kinds of feelings may well develop. True love is always acting on the other person's behalf—for their good—as God does for us. Love is a choice and an action. The Greek word *Agape* is most often translated as *love* in the Bible. In Greek the letter "A" that begins many words is a negative prefix. *A–Gape* literally means *no*–gap, *no*–separation, or *no*–distance. In the original it is a picture word best displayed in Jesus' story of the Prodigal Son. When the son returns home, the father, watching and waiting for that day, runs to him and embraces him. The gap that had existed between them was now gone. That embrace exemplifies *A–Gape*/love.

Whatever we do for others, we should do out of that same embracing and forgiving love for God and for our fellow man, to glorify God with our love. If we're not attending church to glorify God, we are wasting our time. If we're not giving of our time and our money to glorify God, we are wasting our time. If we're not working, playing, worshiping to glorify God, we are wasting our time. We glorify God by loving others in the same way that God first loved us.

> Dear friends, we must love each other because love comes from God. Everyone who loves has been born from God and knows God. The person who doesn't love doesn't know God, because God is love. God has shown us his love by sending his only Son into the world so that we could have life through him. This is love: not that we have loved God, but that he loved us and sent his Son to be the payment for our sins. Dear friends, if this is the way God loved us, we must also love each other. (1 John 4:7–11)

Right after the attack on America on Sept. 11, 2001, many Americans banded together and directed their hatred towards the terrorists and rebels in Afghanistan and Iraq. Despite the hatefulness of the terrorists, God doesn't want us to return hate with hate. He still requires us to love the sinner while hating sin. Prejudice is a form of hate (as well as of pride) that often leads to violence. Cultures that accept and promote wide-spread prejudice of another race, culture, or religion breed hate and violence among themselves as well as those to whom their hatred is directed. It is human nature for people to want to be with people like themselves, but it is not God's nature. God expects us to love *all* people, which comes easily once we've made the Great Exchange.

Racism

Hatred of a particular race or culture angers God. Jesus told his disciples to preach the gospel to everyone in every part of the world.

> He said, "So wherever you go, make disciples of all nations: Baptize them in the name of the Father, and of the Son, and of the Holy Spirit." (Matt. 28:19)

People of every race and nation will be represented in heaven—*all* nations. If you are unable to have relationships with a particular culture of people on earth, how do you expect to have relationships with them in heaven? God expects us to love all people, not just those who are similar in appearance to us or who practice the same customs as we do.

> After these things I saw a large crowd from every nation, tribe, people, and language. No one was able to count how many people there were. (Rev. 7:9)

I was visiting the home of an elderly woman when her doorbell rang. She answered the door, looked at the child on the porch and called back to me, "Judi, please help me. There's a colored boy on my porch. You know how to talk to those people. See what he wants."

Standing on her porch was a ten-year-old African-American boy selling candy bars. The woman's words stung. The boy looked like he was ready to cry, and I was so embarrassed for the woman that for once I was at a loss for words.

This woman, who professes to be a Christian and claims she has no prejudices, would not speak to a young child selling candy bars because he was black. She said she "didn't know how to talk to those people." If she truly saw him as a person loved and created by God, she would have been able to talk with him as she would any of God's children, child or adult. Through her prejudice, she never saw the boy at all. All she saw was a color. Thank God that prejudice and hatred don't exist in heaven, because those who are prejudiced and full of hate won't be there.

God detests any kind of racism, but he is particularly angered by anti–Semitism. The Jews are God's chosen people, and he tells us he will bless the nations and individuals who bless the Jews and curse those who curse the Jews. Martin Luther died shortly after writing an anti–Semitic tract. The United States has gone through two wars and many natural disasters since our presidents have been pressuring Israel to give up land promised to them by God (see Genesis 15:18–21). Coincidences? God still has a plan for his chosen people (see Romans 9–11), and if you come against God's chosen people, you're in big trouble.

Hezbollah terrorists kidnapped a young Israeli soldier in the summer of 2006. When Israel retaliated and attacked Hezbollah fighters, the media portrayed Israel as the bad guys. God's wrath will come upon those journalists and others who slander and bear false witness against the Jews. It is extremely important that they repent of their anti–Semitism and report the truth about God's chosen people.

> I will bless those who bless you, and whoever curses you, I will curse. Through you every family on earth will be blessed. (Gen. 12:3)

People commit lots of sins in the name of their god or for their religious ideals. While Islam claims to be a religion of peace, the hatred and bloodshed between the Sunni and Shiia populations shows all of us that their notion of peace must be when the other side is dead, then you'll have peace. The orthodox Islamists take the Quran very seriously when they are urged to kill Christians and Jews. Since 1948, when the United Nations granted displaced Jews a homeland, Syria has vowed that the solution to the Arab/Jewish conflict is to wipe Israel and the Jews off the face of the earth. Christians cannot support this hatred of the Jews but must take a stand on their behalf!

Expressing love

It is *not* the thought that counts. Just thinking about loving someone doesn't count at all. We need to show our love to others in words and in deeds. It's really sad to think someone could go through his whole life without ever having told the people he loves that he loves them.

*Walt is an elderly gentleman who reads the Bible daily, never misses church, prays at every meal, and even presents his tithes and offerings to God. Despite all these pious acts, Walt has never told his two grown sons or his four grandchildren that he loves them.

Walt was hospitalized, and things didn't look good for him. His older son saw his father lying in the hospital bed and took the opportunity to tell his father for the very first time that he loved him. Walt did not, would not, or could not say the words, "I love you, too, son." You may be nodding now and thinking, "Yeah, I know someone like that. Guess Walt's just from that old generation."

It doesn't matter what generation you're from. Christians show their love to each other, and they also express their love with kind words, which may include saying, "I love you." Walt has never used kind words to his children or grandchildren—words like, "I'm proud of you." "You did a nice job." "I'll miss you." "You're a great father."

When Walt went to his grandson's Kindergarten graduation ceremony, instead of saying, "I'm proud of you," he complained about the color of the robes. When he attended his granddaughter's dance recital, instead of saying, "You did a great job," he complained that the dancers were dancing to Christian music. Seldom has this man who calls himself a Christian ever uttered kind words to anyone, but often has he expressed hatred and disdain for just about everything.

Walt may have expressed his love for his children and grandchildren or his pride in them to other people, but it would be even better if he actually had expressed his love to them personally. It wouldn't leave them wondering whether their father/grandfather loves them or not. God wants us to show and tell the people in our lives that we love them. Jesus came right out and said the words, "I love you." They are words everyone needs to hear. Please tell those you love that you love them before it's too late.

> Jesus said, I have loved you the same way the Father has loved me. So live in my love. If you obey my commandments, you will live in my love. I have obeyed my Father's commandments, and in that way I live in his love. I have told you this so that you will be as joyful as I am, and your joy will be complete. Love each other as I have loved you. This is what I'm commanding you to do. The greatest love you can show is to give your life for your friends. You are my friends if you obey my commandments. I don't call you servants anymore, because a servant doesn't know what his master is doing. But I've called you friends because I've made known to you everything that I've heard from my Father. You didn't choose me, but I chose you. I have appointed you to go, to produce fruit that will last, and to ask the Father in my name to give you whatever you ask for. Love each other. This is what I'm commanding you to do. (John 15:9–17)

Those who hate others, including those who hate homosexuals, murderers, terrorists, adulterers, etc., as well as those who don't love others or won't love others or are incapable of loving others, will not inherit the kingdom of heaven. Hatred is a sin of the mind and soul when you wish great harm on someone or wish that the object of your scorn were dead. That's why John, author of one of the gospels, could say that if you hate your brother, you are a murderer.

If in your heart you know you need to and are ready to repent of hatred, discord, dissensions, factions, or fits of rage and step into the faith life of love, please pray this prayer.

Dear Father, please forgive me for my hatefulness. Help me to control my temper and to stop stirring up trouble. Help me to love as Jesus loved. Help me to choose to express verbally and with my actions my love to others. Help me to love all people regardless of their race, culture, religion, gender, or disability. I accept Jesus as my Lord and Savior and know he forgives my sins of hatefulness and all my sins. I look forward to the day when he will return to take me and all believers to heaven to live with you forever in your glorious kingdom. In Jesus' name I pray. Amen.

8

The Homosexuals

They knew God but did not praise and thank him for being God. Instead, their thoughts were total nonsense, and their misguided minds were plunged into darkness. While claiming to be wise, they became fools. They exchanged the glory of the immortal God for statues that looked like mortal humans, birds, animals, and snakes. For this reason God allowed their lusts to control them. As a result, they dishonor their bodies by sexual perversion with each other. These people have exchanged God's truth for a lie. So they have become ungodly and serve what is created rather than the Creator, who is blessed forever. Amen! For this reason God allowed their shameful passions to control them. Their women have exchanged natural sexual relations for unnatural ones. Likewise, their men have given up natural sexual relations with women and burn with lust for each other. Men commit indecent acts with men, so they experience among themselves the punishment they deserve for their perversion. (Rom. 1:21–27)

As I wrote in the Introduction, this book wasn't written to offend anyone but to set them free. *No one* is without sin; all are in need of Jesus' atoning blood, and no sin is worse than any other except for the unforgivable sin of blaspheming the Holy Spirit. (Matt. 12:31) I want to make it clear that neither God nor I am saying homosexual behavior is the worst sin or is an unforgivable sin, as I have heard some church people say. But homosexual behavior is outside of God's plan for his people, and it needs to be dealt with by Jesus' blood and Holy Spirit power.

Call it whatever you like—sexual preference, sexual orientation, sexually challenged, whatever—God *did not* create anyone to be homosexual. God created man and woman to show his character, personality, and glory when joined in one flesh (marriage). Neither gender fully represents God by itself. God created human beings in his image, and everything God created was very good. Man's rebellion against God is what caused homosexual sin and every other sin to come into the world. People can be set free from homosexual behavior as from every other bondage to sin, through faith in Jesus Christ, being made new creatures by the power of the Holy Spirit, and by making the Great Exchange, exchanging your life for Christ's life lived in you.

Several studies involving twins have attempted to prove that homosexuality is a genetic or biological condition that can't be changed. The studies cite a few cases in which both twins are homosexual, concluding that since twins share identical DNA, homosexuality must be genetic. The truth is that unless *all* homosexual twins have a twin who is also homosexual, then this sin is not a genetic condition since *all* identical twins share the exact same DNA. There are many sets of identical twins in which one twin is heterosexual and the other is homosexual. Thus there is no possible way homosexuality could be a genetic or inherited condition.[1] Homosexuality is exactly what God says it is: sexual immorality or sin.

> Never have intercourse with a man as with a woman. It is disgusting. (Lev. 18:22)

The American Psychology Association removed homosexual behavior from its list of mental disorders in 1973, taking the politically correct position that treatment for homosexual behavior is ineffective because "homosexuals are born that way." After being confronted by thousands of ex–homosexuals who are now heterosexual and over seventy–five psychologists who have successfully treated homosexuals who desired to be heterosexual, Gerald Koocher, president of the American Psychology Association stated, "The APA has no conflict with psychologists who help those distressed by unwanted homosexual attraction."[2] Yes, homosexuals can become happy heterosexuals, as God created them to be and as many already have.

Homosexual Christians

I have heard it said by many that one cannot be a Christian and also be a homosexual. That statement is absolutely not true! Homosexuals who buy into this myth believe they can't be a Christian, so they fall deeper into the sin of homosexual behavior. Or they join a church in which homosexual behavior isn't considered a sin and remain in bondage to homosexual sin. Or they try to fight their homosexual leaning with celibacy while their hearts remain unhealed. None of these things will get them any closer to inheriting the kingdom of heaven. Only by accepting Jesus Christ as your Lord and Savior and by making the Great Exchange can you be delivered from the bondage of homosexual sins.

> A time will come when people will not listen to accurate teachings. Instead, they will follow their own desires and surround themselves with teachers who tell them what they want to hear. People will refuse to listen to the truth and turn to myths. (2 Tim. 4:3–4)

Just because someone calls himself a pastor and leads a church doesn't mean he has been called by the Triune God. Ministers who preach that homosexual behavior is not a sin are not preaching God's Word and are leading many homosexuals astray by giving them a false sense of security about their eternal destination. Most pastors who are pro–homosexual behavior have thrown out most of the gospel along with God's commands to not engage in homosexual behavior. God's Word is the same yesterday, today, and tomorrow. It never changes. If a pastor is contradicting or ignoring what God has already said in the Bible, then he is not speaking for God. God warns about these false teachers.

> False prophets were among God's people in the past as false teachers will be among you. They will secretly bring in their own destructive teachings. They will deny the Lord, who has bought them, and they will bring themselves swift destruction. Many people will follow them in their sexual freedom and will cause others to dishonor the way of truth. In their greed they will use good–sounding arguments to exploit you. The verdict against them from long ago is still in force, and their destruction is not asleep.
>
> God didn't spare angels who sinned. He threw them into hell, where he has secured them with chains of darkness and is holding them for judgment.
>
> These false teachers are dried–up springs. They are a mist blown around by a storm. Gloomy darkness has been kept for them. They arrogantly use nonsense to seduce people by appealing to their sexual desires, especially to sexual freedom. They seduce people who have just escaped from those who live in error. They promise these people freedom, but they themselves are slaves to corruption. A person is a slave to whatever he gives in to. (2 Pet. 2:1–4, 17–19)

The recent acceptance of homosexuality in our society has led many homosexuals to further embrace the myth that their unnatural sexual lusts are not a sin. It wouldn't matter if 99 percent of society believed homosexuality is not a sin. God says it is, and he is the one who will be the judge of who enters heaven and who doesn't. God clearly says that those who engage in homosexual behavior will not inherit the kingdom of God, a place of holiness. (1 Cor. 6:10)

Satan wants homosexuals to attend a church where homosexual intercourse isn't considered a sin. It gives him a firmer grip on the homosexual. He wants homosexuals to believe they can't embrace Christ while they are still in bondage to sin. Satan wants all homosexuals to be in hell with him, and he is going to take as many with him as he can. He's using false teachers and churches that have strayed from God's Word to do it.

A minister in Oklahoma is a prime example of a false teacher. The once popular televangelist was the leader of a large congregation in Tulsa. He preached the gospel of salvation through faith in Jesus Christ. A few years ago, he rejected God's Word and began preaching that all will go to heaven, regardless of whether they accept Christ, regardless if they engage in homosexual sin, regardless of anything.[3]

This minister didn't hear from God; he heard from Satan. The devil loves to attack ministers because he will usually gain not just one soul, but a whole flock of souls. If anyone, regardless of their status, tells you something which goes against what God has already said in the Bible, then it didn't come from God. God's Word doesn't change with the times. The road to heaven is narrow, and few find it. This minister is leading his followers down the very wide, all-inclusive road to hell.

Deliverance takes time

Don't believe that just because you become a Christian, you will immediately be delivered from the bondage of homosexuality. This is one reason many who call themselves Christians don't believe a homosexual can be a Christian—because most homosexuals don't automatically become heterosexual the moment they accept Christ. There are thousands and thousands of ex-homosexuals living happy, God-pleasing lives, which destroys the theory that homosexuality is a genetic condition with which a person is born.

Star Burch, author of *Lord, Take Me and Make Something Beautiful*, was delivered from lesbianism about a year after she accepted Christ and turned her will and life over to him.[4] Some have experienced much longer journeys and others much shorter journeys in their deliverance from this sin. Jesus can and will change hearts and can and will deliver the homosexual from unnatural sexual lusts, but it may or may not happen overnight. It takes years to develop a homosexual mindset and orientation; sometimes it takes years to heal one. When you sincerely accept Jesus as your Savior, the Holy Spirit will come into your heart to help you resist the devil's temptations to do evil and will give you a new life in

Christ. The healing process will begin, and you *will* eventually be delivered from homosexuality.

Many think that if Jesus could really deliver from the bondage of homosexuality, then the moment a person says, "I'm saved! I'm born again in Christ!" then all the sin and garbage in his or her life disappears. This is merely the beginning of God's process of continually working to clean up our hearts as the Great Exchange manifests more and more in our lives. Be assured that Christ died for *all* our sins, including homosexual sins, and that his resurrection power is sufficient to break every hold of Satan.

> I am crucified with Christ: nevertheless I live; yet not I, but Christ liveth in me: and the life which I now live in the flesh I live by the faith of the Son of God, who loved me, and gave himself for me. (Gal. 2:20 KJV)

One of the problems encountered in delivering homosexuals from their sin is that Christian homosexuals and churches that teach that homosexual intercourse is not a sin often reason that since Jesus never spoke about homosexuality in the New Testament, and since Jesus obeyed all the laws of the Old Testament for us, then we don't have to obey them. However, Paul says that every word in the Old Testament is useful for our instruction.

> Every scripture passage is inspired by God. All of them are useful for teaching, pointing out errors, correcting people, and training them for a life that has God's approval. (2 Tim. 3:16)

> First you must understand this: No prophecy in scripture is a matter of one's own interpretation. No prophecy ever originated from humans. Instead, it was given by the Holy Spirit as humans spoke under God's direction. (2 Pet. 1:19–21)

Although Jesus didn't personally speak out against homosexuality, Paul did. (1 Corinthians 6:9, 1 Timothy 1:10) Jesus said his disciples would speak the truth as it would be given to them by the Holy Spirit. Thus Paul's statements about homosexuality are to be considered as coming, not from himself or from his own mind, but from the Holy Spirit. He spoke and wrote the words given to him by God through the Holy Spirit.

> Jesus said to his disciples, When the Spirit of Truth comes, he will guide you into the full truth. He won't speak on his own. He will speak what he hears and will tell you about things to come. He will give me glory, because he will

> tell you what I say. Everything the Father says is also what I say. That is why I said, 'He will take what I say and tell it to you.' (John 16:13–15)
>
> I want you to know, brothers and sisters, that the Good News I have spread is not a human message. I didn't receive it from any person. I wasn't taught it, but Jesus Christ revealed it to me. (Gal. 1:12)

We can't select what to accept and believe from the Bible since every word in the Bible has been breathed by God. The Bible tells us that *unrepentant* homosexual sinners will spend eternity in hell. Many so-called Christians today are telling homosexuals that if they "believe" in Jesus, they will go to heaven. Don't be fooled. They don't understand the word "believe." Belief is not merely intellectual assent, but it is heart and life change resulting in *action* that reflects the belief.

Does God expect you to change your life and clean yourself up only in your own strength? No! That's why he sent Jesus—to break the power of sin in your life. He also offers us His Holy Spirit to help us live our new life in him each day. According to Paul in Romans 12 and Ephesians 4–6, God expects you to change and to not blame God if you don't change!

> We are sure that we know Christ if we obey his commandments. The person who says, "I know him," but doesn't obey his commandments is a liar. The truth isn't in that person. But whoever obeys what Christ says is the kind of person in whom God's love is perfected. That's how we know we are in Christ. Those who say that they live in him must live the same way he lived. (1 John 2:3–6)

Just because something is legal doesn't make it right in God's eyes. If every state legalizes homosexual marriages, domestic partnerships, or homosexual unions, and if no one is ever allowed to speak out against homosexuality again, unrepentant homosexuals will still go to hell when they die. It doesn't matter if they are a Catholic priest, an Episcopalian Bishop, or whosoever. God's Word doesn't change with man's laws. Man can call homosexual behavior whatever he wants; God still calls it sin.

Cross dressers

> A woman must never wear anything men would wear, and a man must never wear women's clothes. Whoever does this is disgusting to the Lord your God. (Deut. 22:5)

The Homosexuals 67

People with gender confusion often have suffered emotional, sexual, or physical abuse, neglect, or lack of nurture. Their basic need for appropriate love and approval from both parents, male and female, has not been met. As a result, some turn to cross dressing to meet emotional needs.

Many transvestites and drag queens are not homosexual, but they are lacking a healthy male spirit. God created men to show his "manly" qualities—faithfulness, love, strength, provider for the family, and head of the household. When men try to act like or look like women, they deny God's purpose in creating them. God wants to restore every man's maleness.

*Don was a cross–dresser for ten years and says that the tendencies went all the way back to his childhood. He began attending a Bible study and, within three months, confessed Jesus as his Lord and Savior. Two months after that, God completely delivered him from cross dressing. The Holy Spirit brought him under conviction of his sin. Don fell down before the Lord, weeping, and called out for deliverance. Within two days, he had thrown away eighteen trash bags of women's clothes and accessories. (He had read in the book of Jude that we should not just hate the sin, but we should also hate the clothes we were wearing when we committed that sin because they might have unclean spirits attached to them.) He told his mentor, "I feel so much better now. I feel like a huge weight has been lifted off of me." Don is enjoying his maleness now.

> And others save with fear, pulling *them* out of the fire; hating even the garment spotted by the flesh. (Jude:23)

God created women to show his "feminine" qualities—appreciation for beauty, nurturing, helping. Women who turn to lesbianism or dress and act like men often do so because they have been abused or pushed around as women. They don't want to be in a submissive position. Sometimes they dress like men because they believe that with their body type and physical appearance they can never be "pretty" no matter what they do. They have given up on their femininity. God wants every woman to know she is loved and to feel beautiful.

God's plan for men and women is that a husband loves and nurtures his wife, and that a wife respects, loves, and supports her husband. In this plan, both men and women are free to help each other be all they can be. When a Godly wife is accepting of a second rank in the family order, she really gets the best part of the deal. The man, as head of the household, is responsible for the family; the woman's burden is lighter! Never think that God doesn't love his daughters.

Katie tells how when she was learning Godly acceptance of the second ranking position in the family (as a major would outrank a lieutenant), to her husband, who wasn't even a Christian, God did amazing things. First, she learned that being submissive was not the same as being a doormat. It simply meant not arguing or insisting on her own way. Whenever her husband was wrong, she learned to give her opinion or suggestion *one time* and then *be quiet*. Every time, she saw God change her husband's mind within a short period of time. She learned that she could trust God to take care of everything and that she never needed to get in strife with her husband. Being submissive to her husband set her free; it didn't put her into more bondage.

Finally, in case you were wondering after reading the Bible passage above ... must women always wear dresses? Of course not. Dresses are not the only form of women's clothing any more than suits make up a man's entire wardrobe. Women's slacks and blouses are made for women and men's pants and shirts for men.

Sex change operations

Those who grow up thinking God made a mistake, that they are really a man in a woman's body or vice versa, are wrong. God doesn't make mistakes. If your body is male, then you have a male spirit. If your body is female, then you have a female spirit. Changing your body to coincide with deceptive thoughts and feelings from the devil is a lot more complicated than turning your life over to God and asking him to restore your true spirit and soul, which he created. Changing the outside without addressing the problems on the inside won't lead to happiness. This defiant action is a slap in the face to a loving God who has chosen gender roles for us just for this life since we will not be married or given in marriage in the new creation. (Gen. 1:27)

> Don't you know that you are God's temple and that God's Spirit lives in you? If anyone destroys God's temple, God will destroy him because God's temple is holy. You are that holy temple! (1 Cor. 3:16–17)

You are God's creation, and all of God's creations are good. If you are battling with gender identity, turn the issue over to God. Jesus can and will deliver you from this tormenting spirit if you accept him as your Lord and Savior and make the Great Exchange. He will change your heart and heal you of the bondage associated with gender identity confusion. If you have already had the sex change operation, you can repent and ask God's forgiveness for destroying his temple. He will forgive and heal you.

If you are a transvestite or are confused about your gender identity, and you want God to heal and restore you, you can say this prayer.

Dear Father, please forgive me for all my sins. I receive Jesus' shed blood as the atonement for my sin. I have been looking in the wrong places for help with my problem, and I know that apart from you I can't change anything. Now I am asking you to change and heal my heart, restore my maleness/femaleness and bring about your plan for my life. Please remove thoughts of transvestitism/gender change from my mind. Help me to walk with you daily and to be patient as you transform me. I accept Jesus as my Lord and Savior and look forward to the day when he will return to take me and all believers to heaven to live with you forever in your glorious kingdom. In Jesus' name I pray. Amen.

If in your heart you know you need to and are ready to repent of the sin of homosexual behavior and of other perverted behaviors and accept Jesus as your Lord and Savior, you can say this prayer.

Dear Father, please forgive me for thoughts, words, and deeds involving homosexuality. Forgive me for seeking sexual gratification with those of my own gender. I want to give up homosexual sin because I know it's an abomination to you. Please help me to resist the devil, the world, and my own sinful flesh when they tempt me and put those lusts in my head. Fill me with your Holy Spirit and deliver me completely from the bondage of homosexual sins of thought, actions, and imaginations. Help me to be patient as you change my heart, heal me, restore my maleness/femaleness, and bring about your plan for my life. I accept Jesus as my Lord and Savior and look forward to the day when he will return to take me and all believers to heaven to live with you forever in your glorious kingdom. In Jesus' name I pray. Amen.

Those who would like more information about deliverance from homosexuality can contact Exodus International, where they'll find help and many testimonies of deliverance.

Exodus International
P.O Box 540119
Orlando, FL 32854
(407) 599–6872
www.exodus–international.org

9

The Idolaters

Worship the Lord your God, fear him, obey his commands, listen to what he says, serve him, and be loyal to him. (Deut. 13:4)

Let's get one thing straight: All gods are not the same. All gods are not the one and only true Triune God. Don't be fooled.

A woman who is involved with New Age religion told me, "We all worship the same God. Buddha, Mohammad, and all the different gods of the Hindu religion—they're all the same god; they just have different names. All of these different religions really worship the same god we do." This statement is absolutely, positively *not true!*

The true God is the Creator of heaven and earth. He spoke, and the Word—his only begotten Son, Jesus, brought forth all things into existence. God the Holy Spirit turned non–living created matter into living things by inspiring life into them. This three–aspect God that the Bible reveals is the one true God. No other gods fit this description. No other gods have died that their creation might live.

Religions built around all other gods describe the need to appease those gods by "good works." Only the God of the Bible gives his creation his own holiness through the atoning blood of his Son. In fact, there is no god but the Triune God. All other supernatural beings are either God's holy angels, who serve him and his people, or they are demonic spirits who masquerade as "gods" and seek to bring bondage and destruction on God's creation.

> We know that the false gods in this world don't really exist and that no god exists except the one God. People may say that there are gods in heaven and on earth—many gods and many lords, as they would call them. But for us, there is only one God, the Father. Everything came from him, and we live for him. There is only one Lord, Jesus Christ. Everything came into being through him, and we live because of him. (1 Cor. 8:4–6)

The God of Christianity is a loving, forgiving God who seeks to have a close personal relationship with each person. No other religion has a loving, personal god. No other religion offers a god who himself provides the way of salvation instead of demanding sacrifices and works of appeasement.

Other so-called gods, such as the god of the Quran, condone beating and torturing women, murdering those who don't accept Islam, and other things that the true God abhors. These are not God's thoughts and ways, but man's. Allah tells believers to hate and kill their enemies; the true Triune God tells believers to love and forgive their enemies. The gods of Islam, Hinduism, Buddhism and other non-Christian religions are not God the Three-in-One Father, Son, and Holy Spirit.

Worshiping any god or gods other than the true Triune God is idolatry. However, just as diabolical are those who don't serve any god. It takes a lot more faith to be an atheist than it does to have faith in God. You need to choose today to make the Great Exchange and to honor and serve God the Father of Jesus, because he's the only true God and the only God who can save you from the torments of hell and grant you entrance into heaven.

Worshiping statues

Recently in India word spread that statues of the Hindu god, Lord Ganesha, were sipping teaspoonfuls of milk. Thousands and thousands of Hindus lined up outside temples across the region to feed these wood, bronze, and marble statues and seek blessings. They called the feeding frenzy a "miracle."[1]

This god they're worshiping and "feeding" is a statue, a man-made idol which someone created with his hands! Before it was a "god," it was a hunk of wood or metal. I won't even debate the "miracle" of whether the statues "drank" the milk or whether it evaporated or was absorbed by the statue, or the fact that believers were tipping their spoons toward the statues, rather than allowing the statues to actually "drink" the milk. It's not important. What's important is that the statue is a statue; it's not a living god!

The God of Christianity is alive! Jesus died and rose from the dead. We can talk to him anytime we want, and he will answer! Not only can he sip a teaspoonful of milk if he's thirsty, but it doesn't have to be fed to him. He's not a piece of metal. He can cry real tears and probably is when he witnesses all the worshipping of statues.

Woe to those of any religion who reject Jesus' atoning death on the cross for their sins in favor of a statue that drinks milk, cries, or bleeds, or any statue for that matter. The Lord's anger is upon them, and it is curses they will receive rather than blessings.

> I am the Lord your God, who brought you out of slavery in Egypt. Never have any other god. Never make your own carved idols or statues that represent any creature in the sky, on the earth, or in the water. Never worship them or serve them, because I, the Lord your God, am a God who does not tolerate rivals. I punish children for their parents' sins to the third and fourth generation of those who hate me. But I show mercy to thousands of generations of those who love me and obey my commandments. (Ex. 20:2–6)

The above passage was so important to God that he made it the very First Commandment—not the fifth, eighth, tenth—but the *first!* Some religions that claim to be Christian have removed these words from Exodus 20 about idolatry from their list of the Ten Commandments. People want to worship and bow down to something they can see. Just because we can't see Jesus doesn't mean he isn't alive and able to communicate with us. He tells us he is with us always, even until the end of time.

God doesn't want us to bow down before *statues* of Jesus or Mary (the mother of Jesus), saints, or any other idols. Those people are not residing in statues. God wants us to worship him, not a piece of wood made in his likeness.

Praying to dead people

Some people who call themselves Christians commit idolatry by praying to dead people. God gets angry when we pray to Mary the mother of Jesus, to the disciples, to angels, to certain saints, to our dead relatives, or to anyone other than him. Jesus tells us to pray to our Heavenly Father in his name—that is, we understand that God's promises to us are delivered through his Son.

> Jesus said, I am the way, the truth, and the life. No one goes to the Father except through me. (John 14:6)

Jesus *never* said you can come to the Father through Mary, angels, the disciples, particular saints, or anyone other than him. An angel became angry with John when John bowed to worship the angel, directing him to worship God instead.

> I, John, heard and saw these things. When I had heard and seen them, I bowed to worship at the feet of the angel who had been showing me these

things. He told me, "Don't do that! I am your coworker. I work with other Christians, the prophets, and those who follow the words in this book. Worship God!" (Rev. 22:8–9)

So what happens when we pray to someone other than God? Nothing happens. That's right, nothing! These people—Mary, Peter, Michael, Paul, Francis of Assisi, Christopher, Anthony, various popes—are not empowered to answer our prayers. Only the one true God hears and answers prayer. The one to whom you pray is the one you worship. So if you are praying to anyone but God, not only are you wasting your breath, but you are angering God by worshiping idols.

Idolaters will find themselves in the fiery lake of burning sulfur. (Rev. 21:20)

Satan, then, does want you to pray to anyone or anything *but* God. He doesn't want you to worship God or confess Jesus as your Savior. He doesn't want you to pray to your Heavenly Father in Jesus' name because he knows those prayers are heard and answered. Mary was born a sinner, just as we all were, as were the disciples and all the people the Roman Catholic Church has canonized (declared to be saints). None of these dead people are able to answer your prayers.

The Catholic Church recently issued a statement claiming that "the Catholic Church alone is the mediator of salvation" and claimed all other faiths are not "full churches" because they don't recognize the primacy of the pope.[2] God considers it idolatry to elevate the pope to the same level as Jesus! The pope is no less a sinner than you or me. The only mediator between Christians and God is Jesus Christ. No one gets to the Father except through Jesus, not even the pope. The pope is no different than the president of any other Christian denomination. Some Catholics must stop the idolatry of worshiping this man or praying to dead popes!

> Everyone who believes has God's approval through faith in Jesus Christ. There is no difference between people. Because all people have sinned, they have fallen short of God's glory. (Rom. 3:22–23)

Thanks to Jesus, we have all been sanctified (made holy in God's eyes) through his death and resurrection, and we have all been made saints. Just because someone may have lived a holier life than another person doesn't make him any more saintly than the next Christian. Paul referred to the Ephesians and the Corinthians as saints, calling them "holy and without blame."

> Paul, an apostle of Jesus Christ by the will of God, to the saints which are at Ephesus, and to the faithful in Christ Jesus: Grace be to you, and peace, from God our Father, and from the Lord Jesus Christ. Blessed be the God and Father of our Lord Jesus Christ, who hath blessed us with all spiritual blessings in heavenly places in Christ: According as he hath chosen us in him before the foundation of the world, that we should be holy and without blame before him in love: Having predestinated us unto the adoption of children by Jesus Christ to himself, according to the good pleasure of his will, To the praise of the glory of his grace, wherein he hath made us accepted in the beloved. In whom we have redemption through his blood, the forgiveness of sins, according to the riches of his grace; Wherein he hath abounded toward us in all wisdom and prudence; Having made known unto us the mystery of his will, according to his good pleasure which he hath purposed in himself: That in the dispensation of the fullness of times he might gather together in one all things in Christ, both which are in heaven, and which are on earth; even in him: (Eph. 1:1–10 KJV)

None of us are deserving of heaven, but we're all holy and righteous through the blood of Jesus and his imputed righteousness. The only one who was born without sin was Jesus. He is the only one who is able to save, serve, and deliver us. He was born without sin but became sin for us so we could have eternal life with him in heaven. No one gets to the Father, through prayer or through death, except through Jesus Christ.

> "Don't be afraid," Samuel told the people. "You did do all these evil things. But don't turn away from the Lord. Instead, serve the Lord wholeheartedly. Don't turn away to follow other gods. They can't help or rescue you, because they don't exist. (1 Sam. 12:20–22)

> Jesus said, I will do anything you ask the Father in my name so that the Father will be given glory because of the Son. If you ask me to do something, I will do it. (John 14:13–14)

> He fills the needs of those who fear him. He hears their cries for help and saves them. The Lord protects everyone who loves him, but he will destroy all wicked people. (Ps. 145:19–20)

> When you call to me, I will answer you. I will be with you when you are in trouble. I will save you and honor you. I will satisfy you with a long life. I will show you how I will save you. (Ps. 91:15–16)

Worshiping people or possessions

It is not always a person, living or dead, who becomes an idol in our lives. Anything that we put ahead of seeking after God and pleasing him is an idol. Some people worship their homes, their cars, alcohol, illegal drugs, prescription pain killers, their spouses or children, their religions or its rituals, their jobs, cherished collections, money, and other material things. Whatever you put ahead of and value more than the Lord Jesus Christ is an idol.

> But first, be concerned about his kingdom and what has his approval. Then all these things will be provided for you. (Matt. 6:33)

> Therefore, put to death whatever is worldly in you: your sexual sin, perversion, passion, lust, and greed (which is the same thing as worshiping wealth). (Col. 3:5)

If you will put God first in your life, the blessings will pour down upon you, and you will know true wealth. Remove any idols from your life, stop praying to anyone or any man–made thing; pray only to Jesus, and allow God to bless you.

> You must serve the Lord your God, and he will bless your food and water. I will take away all sickness from among you. (Ex. 23:25)

God doesn't just request that you worship only him; he commands it with his very First Commandment that you shall have no gods other than him, regardless of who or what those gods represent.

If in your heart you know you need to and are ready to repent of idolatry by worshiping people, false gods, or things, and accept Jesus as your Lord and Savior, you can say this prayer.

Dear Father, forgive me for worshiping other gods. I now can see that lifting anyone or anything higher than their being as created things and calling or acting as if there are other gods besides you is actually idolatry. I believe with all my heart that you are the one and only true Triune God. I know you sent your Son Jesus the Christ/Messiah to die for all my sins and that I have been saved. If I have ever prayed to anyone who has died, thinking that their souls can intercede for me, forgive my foolishness. Thank you for showing me that I need none but Jesus to intercede for me. By your Word and Spirit guide me in this life that I might never put my trust in chemicals to deliver me from the pain and heartbreaks of this Vale of Tears. I will, from this day forward, stop putting people and things ahead of you. I will worship no gods other than you and look forward to the day when your holy angel carries me to Abraham's bosom or when Jesus returns to take me and all believers to heaven to live with you forever in your glorious kingdom. In Jesus' name I pray. Amen.

10

The Immoral

Some people have slipped in among you unnoticed. Not long ago they were condemned in writing for the following reason: They are people to whom God means nothing. They use God's kindness as an excuse for sexual freedom and deny our only Master and Lord, Jesus Christ. (Jude:4)

*Melissa graduated from a Christian elementary school and a Christian high school. She began having sexual relations with a boyfriend at age twelve, had an abortion, began working for an escort service, taking drugs, and lying to her friends and family about her secret life. She married and divorced and continued in prostitution, often with her young daughter in the home.

Melissa was told by a friend that she needed to change her attitude and her behavior or she wouldn't be spending eternity in heaven when she dies. She said, "Yes, I will. I believe Jesus died for me, and I'm forgiven for everything I've done." She said this as she was pushing the friend out of her house so she could engage in prostitution with her next client.

The Bible tells us we should not even associate with a Christian like Melissa who is unwilling to change her heart, mind, and will to please God. God still expects us to hate the sin and love the sinner, but he doesn't want us to associate with immoral people who call themselves Christians. He knows that such a relationship is likely to lead us into sin.

> In my letter to you I told you not to associate with people who continue to commit sexual sins. I didn't tell you that you could not have any contact with unbelievers who commit sexual sins, are greedy, are dishonest, or worship false gods. If that were the case, you would have to leave this world. Now, what I meant was that you should not associate with people who call themselves brothers or sisters in the Christian faith but live in sexual sin, are greedy, worship false gods, use abusive language, get drunk, or are dishonest. Don't eat with such people. After all, do I have any business judging those who are outside the Christian faith? Isn't it your business to judge those who are inside?

God will judge those who are outside. Remove that wicked man from among you. (1 Cor. 5:9–13)

Immoral Christians

This entire book discusses immoral people—liars, adulterers, thieves, and others—who have not accepted Jesus as their only hope for salvation. Many people who say they believe in Jesus still live immoral lives. They think that *saying* they believe is the same thing as actually *believing*. It is true we are saved through faith in Christ alone, and not by any deeds of our own, but to believe on Jesus' name for salvation means to live in trust and obedience to him. If we truly have been born again, then we have made the Great Exchange, exchanging our life for Christ's. We have received the desire and the power to live according to the leading of the Holy Spirit and not according to the desires of the flesh. (Romans 8:5–9)

> I have often told you, and now tell you with tears in my eyes, that many live as the enemies of the cross of Christ. In the end they will be destroyed. Their own emotions are their god, and they take pride in the shameful things they do. Their minds are set on worldly things. (Phil. 3:18–19)

I have heard numerous times from various people that "we can't legislate morality." Let's stop and think about that false propaganda. Actually we can and do legislate morality all the time. I don't know of any jurisdictions that have said stealing is now legal, steal all you want, or kill if you feel like it, or drive drunk. Unfortunately there are many individuals, associations, businesses, and activist groups that persist in trying to legislate immorality. It isn't just immoral individuals whom we need to remove from our lives, but also immoral groups, clubs, and associations that we're supporting financially or by actively or inactively supporting their immoral agendas.

A good example of an immoral organization is the National Education Association (NEA). This teachers' union attacks Christian groups and supports abortion, homosexual behavior, and other sins that lead to eternal damnation.[1] What frightens me the most is that their immoral agenda is directed at our children!

If you're a member of the NEA and are concerned that if you renounce your membership, you'll lose insurance coverage and legal protection, please consider other organizations, such as the Association of American Educators or the Christian Educators Association International, which will provide this coverage to you at about a third of the price you are now paying for NEA coverage. Religious objectors to the immoral agenda of their union also have the option of sending their union dues to a charity rather than financially supporting the objectives of a union they don't agree with. To learn more about your rights as a union member, read the pamphlet by Matthew D. Staver, titled "Union Memberships and its Constitutional Implications."

Ford Motor Company has spent hundreds of thousands of dollars supporting and promoting immoral sexual behavior, including giving money to homosexual organizations, gay pride events, gay media awards, and placing sexually suggestive ads in homosexual magazines.[2] Is this the kind of automobile manufacturer you want to do business with?

We express our own morality or immorality in the company we keep, the organizations we belong to, the businesses we support, and the ideas and issues we back. If we're voting in favor of immoral issues, such as special rights for homosexual sin, abortion, or embryonic stem cell research, or we're voting for candidates who support these immoral issues, then we're guilty of immorality ourselves and need to repent and ask God's forgiveness. For Jesus' sake, God will forgive the disobedient Christian. Martin Luther King, Jr. said, "He who accepts evil without protesting against it is really cooperating with it."

We can't say we believe in morality but then go to the polls and cast a vote for immorality, regardless of what other wonderful issues a candidate might support. Political candidates often try to instill fear in voters to persuade them to vote contrary to their morals. If we're afraid to cast a vote for the moral candidate for fear of losing social security benefits or fear of a terrorist attack, we're being cowardly, not trusting God to provide for us and to protect us. We're putting our trust in someone we know to be immoral, so chances are that he or she could also be a liar, a thief, or worse. The wise choice would be to vote for God, which requires voting for the candidate God would support, not the one we believe might make life easier or better for us.

Let's give the Roman Catholic Church a round of applause for finally starting to crack down on professed Christian politicians in legislatures and the like who have excommunicated themselves for supporting laws favoring sinful acts.

Changing immoral behavior

All sinners can be forgiven, but the Bible tells us not to associate with those who call themselves Christians yet persist in sinning. Their minds are on the world instead of on the Lord Jesus Christ and the glorious eternal future he has planned for us. He will bring the present creation to a flaming end and usher in the New

Creation where his throne will be in the new world. This sin infested earth will be consumed in flames and a new heaven and a new earth will replace it. (Rev. 21:1)

Why should we not associate with these "Christians?" First, maintaining fellowship gives approval to the sin, and this is dangerous for the unrepentant sinner. Second, because all too often the bad apple spoils the barrel instead of the good apples restoring the spoiled.

> You must understand this: In the last days there will be violent periods of time. People will be selfish and love money. They will brag, be arrogant, and use abusive language. They will curse their parents, show no gratitude, have no respect for what is holy, and lack normal affection for their families. They will be reckless and conceited. They will love pleasure rather than God. They will appear to have a godly life, but they will not let its power change them. Stay away from such people. (2 Tim. 3:1–5)

God wants our minds and hearts to be focused on him at all times. When they are, we live in peace and joy. We lose our desire for the things in the world that are sinful and dangerous to our body, soul, mind, and spirit. Immorality has no place in a Christian's life. Yes, we can sin and be forgiven, but we need to stop sinning!

> My dear children, I'm writing this to you so that you will not sin. Yet, if anyone does sin, we have Jesus Christ, who has God's full approval. He speaks on our behalf when we come into the presence of the Father ... Don't love the world and what it offers. Those who love the world don't have the Father's love in them ... the world and its evil desires are passing away. But the person who does what God wants lives forever. (1 John 2:1,15,17)

When we commit the same sin a second, third, or however many times, we run the risk we will stop feeling guilty about that sin, and we give Satan a foothold in our hearts. If we no longer feel guilty about a sin, we don't feel the need to confess, repent, and receive God's mercy and forgiveness.

> Keep your mind on things above, not on worldly things. You have died, and your life is hidden with Christ in God. When Christ appears in your life, then you, too, will appear with him in glory. (Col. 3:2–4)

You say, "I can't change myself; I've tried!" You are probably right—you can't! That's why your loving heavenly Father sent Jesus, not only to pay the penalty for sin, but *to break its power over you*. When you call on his name to save you from sin, not just to save you from the *penalty* for sin, when you declare him to be your Lord, the boss of your life, and you accept his shed blood to cover your sin, then you will have no trouble making the Great Exchange. Jesus will come into your heart and exchange his life for yours, and you will no longer have to fear the penalty for sin.

> You know very well that no person who is involved in sexual sin, perversion, or greed (which means worshiping wealth) can have any inheritance in the kingdom of Christ and of God. (Eph. 5:5)

You can be sure that *nothing* you have done can separate you from God's love and redemption if only you will call on him! Don't wait—his arms are open to you! If in your heart you know you need to and are ready to repent of immorality and receive God's forgiveness, you can say this prayer.

Dear Father, please forgive me for my immoral ways. In particular forgive me for the sins of (name them here). I want to live in obedience to your Word and your commands, but I need your help because I'm weak. Fill me with your Holy Spirit and set me on the right path. I accept Jesus as my Lord and Savior and know that you forgave me for my immorality when Jesus' death on the cross was acceptable as my substitute. Thank you for calling me by the gospel and enlightening me with your free Spirit. Help me to appreciate with a thank-filled heart that all my sins are now gone for Jesus' sake. I look forward to the day when Jesus will return to take me and all believers to heaven to live with you forever in your glorious kingdom. In Jesus' name I pray. Amen.

11

The Impure

Nothing unclean, no one who does anything detestable, and no liars will ever enter it [the heavenly city of Jerusalem]. Only those whose names are written in the Lamb's Book of Life will enter it. (Rev. 21:27)

God tells us that anyone or anything that is not pure won't enter the kingdom of heaven. The Holy Spirit inspired the writers to use at least three different words in the New Testament that are translated as *pure*. *Impure* usually is just the opposite of those words. The English word *pure* comes to us almost directly from the Greek word for fire, (*i.e. pyros*). We still have a funeral *pyre* or *Pyrex* for heat resistant glass. Metals were purified by fire, which is actually redundant in a way. The notion of purgatory (which doesn't exist and is never mentioned in the Bible) came about as a place where impure souls could be burned clean.

The *impure* includes everyone mentioned in this book who has not made the Great Exchange, repented of their sins, and been washed clean by the blood of Jesus. Impurity is similar to immorality but also includes the sin of lust. It also refers to the unapprised, (i.e. still in the original sin of our first parents). Impurity is what results when we give in to the temptation of lust. Impure thoughts are created from lust in the heart, lust of the flesh (sexual), and lust of the eye (envy, covetousness).

Lets go back for a few moments and review. How do temptations become sins of thought? Jesus Christ was tempted in every way, such as we are, yet he did not sin. Temptations can lead to sins of lust and sinful actions. Some people would claim that sins of thought are just as bad as sins of deed. Maybe not. Sins of thought have no social consequences; they stay trapped inside our skulls. It is possible to be impure in thoughts, words, and actions.

God didn't call us to be sexually immoral but to be holy. (1 Thes. 4:7)

> Run away! Run away! Get away from there! Do not touch anything unclean. Get away from it! Make yourselves pure, you Levites who carry the utensils for the Lord's temple. (Is. 52:11)
>
> Blessed are those whose thoughts are pure. They will see God. (Matt. 5:8)
>
> Finally, brothers and sisters, keep your thoughts on whatever is right or deserves praise: things that are true, honorable, fair, pure, acceptable, or commendable. (Phil.4:8)

There are very few, if any, 100 percent pure things in the world. You'll hear about pure silver or gold, pure silk, satin, or wool, or pure cane sugar, to give a few examples. If you look closely, most items which claim to be pure still have at least some minor flaws or impurities. If you've ever gone shopping for diamonds, you probably understand the difficulty in finding a pure and perfect stone. There will always be flaws in the color, cut, or clarity.

We too have flaws and commit sins which keep us from being 100 percent pure. Are any of us pure enough to enter God's kingdom? Jesus says we must become as innocent and pure as a small child to enter heaven and that we must have clean hands, a pure heart, and live according to God's Word in complete trust in and obedience to him.

> He called a little child and had him stand among them. Then he said to them, "I can guarantee this truth: Unless you change and become like little children, you will never enter the kingdom of heaven. Whoever becomes like this little child is the greatest in the kingdom of heaven. (Matt: 18: 2–4)
>
> Who may go up the Lord's mountain? Who may stand in his holy place? The one who has clean hands and a pure heart and does not long for what is false or lie when he is under oath. (Ps. 24:3–4)
>
> How can a young person keep his life pure? He can do it by holding on to your word. (Ps. 119:9)

Becoming pure

No one but Jesus is pure enough to enter heaven, but thanks to Jesus' death on the cross, he has washed us clean with his blood to make us pure enough to enter heaven too. Purity can be obtained only by accepting Jesus as your Lord and Savior. Jesus has made not only us clean and pure through his perfect, sinless life and sacrificial death, but he has made everything around him clean and pure as well.

Where once God's dietary laws labeled foods like pork and shellfish unclean for human consumption, thanks to Jesus' having lived a pure life and having fulfilled all of the Old Testament Law's demands, God now considers those dietary laws to have served their purpose. Foods previously deemed unclean are now pure enough for us to eat.

When St. Peter was called to the home of Cornelius, a Roman Centurion, he received a vision showing how God had changed things because Jesus had fulfilled the laws and dietary restrictions of the Old Testament. Before Peter could go to Cornelius, the Lord sent him a vision of a large sheet coming down from heaven filled with many animals, all unclean by the standards of the Torah. The Lord told him to kill and eat them. (God is not a vegetarian.) Peter had grave reservations about eating unclean, common, or impure flesh. However, God said that whatever God now chooses to call clean and pure, it is now clean and pure. Peter knew then that God considered Cornelius and his family pure, whereas before they were impure (Acts 10). Since Jesus obeyed all the laws of the Old Testament, we're not required to. Some religions still observe the food laws of the Old Testament. Christians, however, know they are not saved by the law but by the gospel.

> Since Christ's blood has now given us God's approval, we are even more certain that Christ will save us from God's anger. (Rom: 5:9)

> Through the blood of his Son, we are set free from our sins. God forgives our failures because of his overflowing kindness. (Eph. 1:7)

> God was pleased to have all of himself live in Christ. God was also pleased to bring everything on earth and in heaven back to himself through Christ. He did this by making peace through Christ's blood sacrificed on the cross. (Col. 1:19–20)

> Jesus Christ, the witness, the trustworthy one, the first to come back to life, and the ruler over the kings of the earth. Glory and power forever and ever belong to the one who loves us and has freed us from our sins by his blood and has made us a kingdom, priests for God his father. Amen. (Rev. 1:5–6)

Jesus is the only one who can remove our impurity and make us clean enough to enter God's kingdom. When we have exchanged our life for his, receiving his sacrificial death to cover our sins and following him as Lord of our life, he will progressively cleanse us from all immorality and impure things in our lives, preparing us for our heavenly destiny.

If in your heart you know you need to and are ready to repent of your impurity and accept Jesus as the only one who can make you pure, you can say this prayer.

Dear Father, please forgive my hidden sins of thoughts with my unholy and impure attitudes. Because of your perfect life and sacrificial death, all of my sins have been forgiven. Jesus, I accept you as my Lord and Savior, knowing you are the one who has made me pure enough to enter your kingdom. Help me to live my life in a way that is pure and pleasing to you. I look forward to the day when Jesus will return to take me and all believers to heaven to live with you forever in your glorious kingdom. In Jesus' name I pray. Amen.

12

The Liars

You must do these things: Speak the truth to each other. Give correct and fair verdicts for peace in your courts. Don't even think of doing evil to each other. Don't enjoy false testimony. I hate all these things, declares the Lord. (Zec. 8:16–17)

Our society has become far too tolerant of liars. We are so used to people lying to us that we almost expect lies from certain segments of our culture, such as advertisers, politicians, and the media. We try to downplay the seriousness of lying by labeling lies as "little lies" or "teensy lies" or "white lies," among other things. We must remember that lying is a damnable sin.

> There are six things that the Lord hates, seven that are disgusting to him: arrogant eyes, a lying tongue, hands that kill innocent people, a mind devising wicked plans, feet that are quick to do wrong, a dishonest witness spitting out lies, and a person who spreads conflict among relatives. (Prov. 6:16–19)

Deception

Let's take a look at how the liar hurts himself and those to whom he tells his lies:

A citizen inflates the legal deductions on his income tax form to gain a few extra dollars on his refund check from the IRS. Or he intentionally fails to report a second income he received in which he was paid cash for odd jobs. Not a big deal. Everyone does it, right? It can't be that big of a sin.

> It is better to be poor than a liar. (Prov. 19:22)

The mistake a lot of people make is believing that because many people do something, that makes it okay. That's why there will be many more people in hell and fewer in heaven. Jesus says, "Give the emperor what belongs to the emperor, and give God what belongs to God." (Matt. 22:21) Cheating on your income tax or on a test or on a spouse—all cheating—is deceptive. Cheating is lying, and it is also a form of stealing in that you're stealing the truth from someone.

> But you, O God, will throw wicked people into the deepest pit. Bloodthirsty and deceitful people will not live out half their days. (Ps. 55:23)

A homeowner falsely fills out the disclosure statement when selling his house, intentionally neglecting to inform buyers that his basement floods during heavy rains.

> You didn't lie to people but to God. (Acts 5:4)

A parent returns a toy to the store, telling the clerk that it never worked when, in fact, her child had broken it.

> Never steal, lie, or deceive your neighbor. (Lev. 19:11)

A worker calls his office, telling his boss he must stay home to care for a sick child when he actually plans to catch an afternoon baseball game.

> I hate lying; I am disgusted with it. (Ps. 119:163)

An unemployment applicant compiles an endless list of companies she has called or visited seeking employment when, in truth, she has not begun to look for a job and won't, if she can get away with it, until her unemployment compensation runs out.

> Keep vanity and lies far away from me. (Prov. 30:8)

A man sells a car to his neighbor without telling him that the engine overheats. When the neighbor returns the car, the man says, "That's funny, it never overheated on me."

> So then, get rid of lies. Speak the truth to each other, because we are all members of the same body. (Eph. 4:25)

As a society we have become so used to people lying to us that we have whole categories of jokes about various professions in which lying is seen as the norm—politicians, journalists, lawyers, used car salesmen, and real estate agents, to name a few. Politicians make all sorts of promises to their would-be constituents to get elected. Journalists lie to readers to sway their opinions on various issues. Lawyers lie to win a case. Car salesmen and real estate agents lie to make a sale.

Liars are cowards. They don't trust God to help them to get elected, or to set an innocent man free, or to make a sale. They rely on deception to advance their positions rather than relying on God, which is one of the reasons God has no tolerance for liars. Let me make it clear that I'm writing about the habitual liar and not the occasional offender, although she too should repent and seek God's forgiveness.

Rich, a real estate agent in St. Louis, refuses to lie in any situation. While other agents might misrepresent a piece of property or falsely inform a buyer who wants to make an offer on a listing that someone else is writing an offer at that very moment, Rich always presents the truth to buyers and sellers. The result for Rich, after twenty-five years of working honestly and ethically, is that God is blessing his agency. He receives a lot of referrals from buyers and sellers, and agents who have worked with him never question his contracts or the information he provides to them about one of his listings. He relies on God to run his agency, not on his own wits or on lies, and he is reaping what he sows.

Gossip

A secretary at a Lutheran church in St. Louis lost her job due partially to rumors and gossip. She had made a comment about a new contemporary church service, saying that because the time it was being held would conflict with the regular church service, it would fail to attract new worshipers. Instead, she said, the church would just be redistributing its members and worship resources between the two services, causing loss of fellowship and unity in the congregation.

A church member gossiped to another member that the secretary was trying to "sabotage the new service." This person then gossiped to another, who repeated the rumor to another. Members then began adding to the rumor. "Well, she also said this to so and so." "And remember when she told this church member about …" Most of the rumors and gossip boiled down to how this secretary had been talking about the Bible and preaching the gospel of Jesus Christ. The problem for some was that she took the Bible more literally than they did. Instead of speaking with the secretary about these issues, the people who had a problem with her just talked to others.

An opinion offered when asked had turned into a horrible crime, just as Satan knew it would when he started the gossip going. The church secretary had given her answer based on her understanding of the gospel. Rumors and gossip had resulted in her removal from the job she had held in the congregation.

> Without wood a fire goes out, and without gossip a quarrel dies down. (Prov. 26:20)

> A devious person spreads quarrels. A gossip separates the closest of friends. (Prov. 16:28)

Rumors and gossip are generally nothing more than half truths, partial truths, and even outright lies. You tend to learn more about the person doing the gossiping than you learn about the person they're gossiping about. The main principle on discussing people with other people is this: If it isn't kind, helpful, positive, or edifying *and* it doesn't *need* to be said, then don't say it.

Dr. Martin Luther tried to give us the antidote for gossip in the close of his explanation for the meaning of the Eighth Commandment, which is "Thou shalt not bear false witness against thy neighbor." Luther said: "… defend, speak well of and put the best construction on everything."

Put the best spin on everything

As Luther said, we should always defend our neighbor and put the best possible construction on their words and actions. When I was marketing my first book, *It Was Never About Books*, I sent over one hundred letters to pastors who had known the minister the book was written about. A few of the pastors had also known me, so to each of them I wrote a more personal letter.

I happened to have a photo of one of the pastors I was writing to, which also included me in the picture, along with about a dozen other people. I thought I'd send it to him to jog his memory as to who I was after thirty years of no contact with him. Since I was standing right next to him in the photo, I cropped the picture to remove others who were in it so that it just showed him and me, making me more easily identifiable. I also included a copy of a letter he had written to me during the same time period. He could have interpreted the letter and photo in a number of different ways. As a pastor, one would think his very first thoughts, his very first reaction would be positive.

When I heard from most of the other pastors but not from him, I emailed him several times. He didn't get back to me until he had learned that a fellow colleague of his had purchased my book. His wife, his grown children, and God only knows how many others in his circle who claim Christ Jesus as their Lord, had interpreted the inclusion of the photo of him and me, along with the old letter, as something "scary," perhaps even a fatal attraction kind of thing. As a writer, I've kept a journal since I was a young teen and have saved nearly every letter and postcard I have ever received (not just his). I have since learned this is a common practice among aspiring writers, who are able to extract ideas from the journals and letters years down the road. The photo I had saved and cropped was an ordinary group shot at a celebration.

Satan had attempted to turn something innocent, constructed with a pure heart, into something unclean. He succeeded by instilling thoughts of fear and condemnation in the pastor and by instilling thoughts of shame and embarrassment in me.

Putting the best spin on another person's words and actions means always giving people "the benefit of the doubt." In this situation, the pastor never gave me the benefit of the doubt. He didn't even recognize doubts that Satan had put in his head. Those thoughts didn't come from the Holy Spirit.

Since mailing the letters to pastors, I have become email friends with several of them, one of whom helped with the writing of this book. I guess it goes without saying that this pastor isn't one of them. My hope is that he will repent of his negative thoughts regarding my motives for contacting him.

Bearing false witness

If you deliberately bear false witness—lie about someone in a negative way in order to gain from it either materially or emotionally—then you are harboring hatred in your heart toward that person. Bearing false witness is a serious sin—so serious, in fact, that God made it one of his Ten Commandments.

A pastor was justly accused of sexual misconduct by a parishioner. Rather than confessing, repenting, and asking for God's forgiveness, he chose to deny the accusations and, in doing so, he bore false witness against the accuser by calling her a liar.

> Never swear by my name in order to deceive anyone. This dishonors the name of your God. I am the Lord. (Lev. 19:12)

A worker is reprimanded by his boss for leaking confidential information to another employee. The worker lies to his boss, telling him it was another employee who gave out the information.

> Never spread false rumors. Don't join forces with wicked people by giving false testimony. (Ex. 23:1)

A driver runs a stop sign and slams into a car traveling through an intersection. When the officer arrives, the driver tells him the accident was the other driver's fault, that *she* had run the stop sign.

> Keep your tongue from saying evil things and your lips from speaking deceitful things. (Ps. 34:13)

The media is often guilty of bearing false witness. One newscaster lost his credibility and was forced into early retirement when he, using documents he probably should have known were forged, attempted to spin a yarn about President George W. Bush's National Guard service. Not only did this journalist disgrace himself and leave the public wondering if there really is such a reality as journalism ethics, but he turned his back on God by revealing himself to be a liar.[1]

Is it ever right to *withhold* the truth? Many police departments are hamstrung in their efforts to arrest criminals because of a "Don't Snitch" mentality on the streets. While it may be justifiable for a physician to withhold the news of a death to a patient in critical condition from the same accident, it is never right to withhold the truth, thereby aiding and abetting a criminal and preventing justice from being served. Withholding the truth is a form of stealing, as well as lying.

Slander

Slander is false witness aimed at someone's professional or personal reputation. It is Satan's work because he is the one whose goal in life is to destroy people. Libel is slandering someone through the written word.

> Jesus said, A thief comes to steal, kill, and destroy. But I came so that my sheep will have life and so that they will have everything they need. (John 10:10)

An elderly patient orders new dentures from her dentist. They don't fit as they should and need to be adjusted. The dentist tells her he'd be happy to adjust them for her. Instead she tells all her friends and neighbors about the poor treatment and product she received from the dentist and advises everyone not to go to him. His practice suffers as a result of her malice.

> Never lie when you testify about your neighbor. (Ex. 20:16)

Tabloids are often guilty of libel, although justice is seldom sought by those libeled because celebrities and those in the public eye must prove that the person acted with actual malice when writing the libelous statement. Intent is very difficult to prove. Some personalities also believe in the old adage that there is no such thing as bad publicity and actually do things to encourage gossip and rumor mongering.

If you know in advance that quite a bit of what tabloids print is false, you should avoid reading them. Many tabloid articles are written for shock appeal and to make a profit, with little or no regard for the impact of the lies on the victims written about. Publishers and reporters of these types of magazines will have to answer to God on judgment day for the damage they caused by disobeying his commandment to not bear false witness against a neighbor.

> A lying witness will not go unpunished. One who tells lies will not escape. (Prov. 19:5)

If in your heart you know you need to and are ready to repent of lying in any form and receive God's forgiveness, you can say this prayer.

Dear Father, I come to you in the name of your Son Jesus Christ, who died so that I and those who are making a habit or lifestyle of lying might come to know you as the Way, the Truth, and the Light. Please forgive me for all the lies I've told in my life. Forgive me for all the times I've gossiped and spread rumors, for the times I have witnessed falsely against another person, and for the times I have slandered someone. Forgive all the lies and deceptions which have been a part of my life. Renew your Spirit within me that I might fight off Satan's deception that telling a lie is the right thing to do. I accept Jesus' death on the cross as the full and perfect atonement for all my sins. I know in my heart that I have been forgiven for his sake. Give me a clean heart and a right spirit so that my conscience is again your pure voice directing me toward your way for living both now and in eternity. Guided by your Spirit I will strive to always be truthful and honest. I accept you as my Lord and Savior and look forward to the day when you'll return for me and all believers and take us to heaven to live with you forever in your glorious kingdom. In Jesus' name I pray. Amen.

13

The Murderers

You come from your father, the devil, and you desire to do what your father wants you to do. The devil was a murderer from the beginning. He has never been truthful. He doesn't know what the truth is. (John 8:44)

Precursors to murder

You don't have to read very far into the Bible to find the first murderer. Cain killed his brother Abel because he was jealous that the Lord favored Abel. The Lord was pleased with Abel because Abel offered him the first fruits of his flock, whereas Cain offered the Lord the rest of his crops after he had taken care of his own needs first. In Cain's case, jealousy had led to murder. Murder is usually preceded by any number of sins.

A closer look at the Fifth Commandment in the original Hebrew, translated, should literally read: "Thou shalt not even have murderous thoughts." Thus God not only forbids the taking of human life but also the will or wish that someone were dead. Another word for that sinful thought is *hate*. Hatred in all its various forms can lead to murder.

Greed and theft can lead to murder. Richard Salinas, an IHOP cook on Staten Island, was robbed and murdered by three men while he was on his way home from work.[1]

Lying can lead to murder. A Utah man murdered his pregnant wife because she discovered he had been lying to her about his acceptance into medical school and was afraid she would expose his lies to everyone.[2]

Anger can lead to murder. A thirteen–year–old boy was angry at his teacher for giving him a failing grade, so he took a gun to school and fatally shot the teacher.[3]

Pride, coveting, and selfish ambitions can lead to murder. A mother was proud of her daughter and wanted her to be on the cheerleading squad. The daughter lacked the talent to make the team. The mother hired a hit man to murder the mother of a girl who did make the squad, hoping the daughter would be so upset at her mother's death she would quit the team, and her own daughter could move into the spot. Thank God she was caught before she could proceed with her murderous plans![4]

Adultery can lead to murder. A woman and her lover hired the lover's cousin to murder her husband.[5]

Envy, coveting, drunkenness, hatred—all kinds of sins and evil thoughts and feelings can lead to murder. We sin in our thoughts, words, and deeds, so just thinking about murdering someone is as bad in God's eyes as committing the actual deed.

> Jesus said, "You have heard that it was said to your ancestors, 'Never murder. Whoever murders will answer for it in court.' But I can guarantee that whoever is angry with another believer will answer for it in court. Whoever calls another believer an insulting name will answer for it in the highest court. Whoever calls another believer a fool will answer for it in hellfire. (Matt. 5:21–22)

> Everyone who hates another believer is a murderer, and you know that a murderer doesn't have eternal life. (1 John 3:15)

Jesus says to love your neighbor as yourself. That is, we are to act on behalf of our neighbor equally as we would act on our own behalf. Lack of love, or hatred, is the seed of murder.

Murderous thoughts

We don't have laws for some of the sins in this book, such as not forgiving others and worshiping idols, but every nation has laws against murder. It is troubling that we even have to make laws against murdering someone. Wouldn't it be great if everyone valued life so much that murder never entered their minds? But how many more murders would there be if there were no laws against it? How many people who have murder in their hearts would go ahead and carry out the deed?

> For example, a person must realize that laws are not intended for people who have God's approval. Laws are intended for lawbreakers and rebels, for ungodly people and sinners, for those who think nothing is holy or sacred, for those who kill their fathers, their mothers, or other people. Laws are intended for people involved in sexual sins, for homosexuals, for kidnappers, for liars, for those who lie when they take an oath, and for whatever else is against accurate teachings. Moses' Teachings were intended to be used in agreement with

the Good News that contains the glory of the blessed God. I was entrusted with that Good News. (1 Tim. 1:9–11)

If you have something against someone, you need to forgive that person or your negative thoughts are likely to turn into bitterness and hatefulness. You might be tempted to act on those thoughts or begin wishing for something harmful to befall another person. You allow Satan to get a foothold in your heart. There is an incredible irony here. When you forgive someone who has wronged you, who does it benefit the most? You! Yes! Did it ever occur to you that the person you're carrying a grudge against doesn't even know you have those ill feelings against him? So forgiveness works, especially for you.

The Greek word that is usually translated forgive actually is a picture word recalling the Great Day of Atonement. On that day two goats were brought before the high priest in Israel. One goat was sacrificed; the other became the scapegoat. The high priest placed the sins of the people upon the scapegoat, and the goat, symbolically carrying the sins of the people, was chased away into the wilderness. The word forgiveness actually means to chase away like the scapegoat in Israel. (Lev. 16:8)

> Whoever says, "I love God," but hates another believer is a liar. People who don't love other believers, whom they have seen, can't love God, whom they have not seen. Christ has given us this commandment: The person who loves God must also love other believers. (1 John 4:20–21)

Never pray to God for something bad to befall someone for any reason; the wicked (those who have not repented of their sin) are already under God's curse. It is God's desire to bless people; that's why he sent Jesus to redeem us from the curse of sin and death. God wants us to pray that those who sin will turn from their sin and believe in Jesus. When you curse someone (wish evil on them), you do the devil's work.

Abortion

Abortion is such a controversial issue that I was hesitant to even cover it in this chapter, but I believe the Holy Spirit has led me to include it. Abortion is the "shedding of innocent blood," which God hates.

> These six things doth the Lord hate: yea, seven are an abomination unto him: A proud look, a lying tongue, and hands that *shed innocent blood*, a heart that devises wicked imaginations, feet that be swift in running to mischief, a false

witness that speaks lies, and he that sows discord among brethren. (Proverbs 6:16–19, KJV, italics mine)

Let scientists and doctors argue about when life begins or when death occurs. As Christians we know all life is created by God. The moment the sperm connects with the egg and fertilizes it, God's work has begun to create new life. He loves the life he has created and has a plan and a purpose for that life. God knew you before you were born.

What really seems strange in the debate about abortion is that untold numbers of people who attend worship and confess one of the three ecumenical creeds during the worship service still have abortions themselves when their lives are not threatened by the continuing pregnancy. What's in those creeds of the Christian churches? That the life of Jesus the Christ/Messiah begins when the Holy Spirit fertilized Mary's ovum. It's called the Incarnation or the becoming flesh. Maybe you've said these words yourself: "... *Who was conceived by the Holy Spirit and born of the virgin Mary* ..." If we tell the world that this is what we believe about Jesus our Lord God and Savior, why is it any different with all other human beings? It isn't any different!

> You alone created my inner being. You knitted me together inside my mother. I will give thanks to you because I have been so amazingly and miraculously made. Your works are miraculous, and my soul is fully aware of this. My bones were not hidden from you when I was being made in secret, when I was being skillfully woven in an underground workshop. Your eyes saw me when I was only a fetus. Every day of my life was recorded in your book before one of them had taken place. (Ps. 139:13–16)

When Mary was pregnant with Jesus, she visited Elizabeth, who was pregnant with John the Baptist. Baby John leapt in his mother's womb when Mary walked into the room and greeted them. Before John was even born, he was able to recognize Jesus' presence in the room!

We might also learn from God here when a woman becomes a mother, and it is not when the child is delivered. Mary is probably no more than two weeks pregnant when Elizabeth calls her "... the mother of my Lord ..." Motherhood, in God's Word and eyes, begins with conception.

> When Elizabeth heard the greeting, she felt the baby kick. Elizabeth was filled with the Holy Spirit. She said in a loud voice, "You are the most blessed of all women, and blessed is the child that you will have. I feel blessed that the

> mother of my Lord is visiting me. As soon as I heard your greeting, I felt the baby jump for joy. (Luke 1:41–44)

Just because something is legal doesn't make it morally right. Slavery was legal at one time. Murdering Jews, the disabled, homosexuals, the mentally ill, and the Gypsies, among others, was legal at one time in Germany. It is legal for homosexuals to marry in at least one state. We know that in God's view this is not a marriage/mating at all. We cannot equate legality with morality. Abortion is legal, but that doesn't make it right. God says we should not purposely take innocent life (murder).

> Murderers will find themselves in the fiery lake of burning sulfur. (Rev.21:8)

I've seen bumper stickers that read, "Catholics for Choice" or "Pro–Choice Christian." A pro–choice Christian is an oxymoron. We can't have it both ways. God says you're either hot or cold; if you're lukewarm, he'll spit you out. Some of the same people who protest cutting down trees, destroying a few bird's eggs, or downsizing the deer population, fight to retain the right to kill unborn babies. The same people who campaign to eliminate the death penalty for premeditated murderers and serial killers, somehow rationalize the killing of the pre–delivered child by promoting the death penalty for the most innocent of all, God's children. Abortion clinics are nothing more than death camps for pre–delivered babies. Tree huggers and animal rights activists should put as much effort into protecting pre–delivered children as they do trying to protect the non–human elements of society. God created and knows all the unborn children, and he has a holy purpose for their lives. It would help us all if we stopped using the word "abortion" and called the act what it most often is, cold–blooded, calculated, pre-meditated murder.

> Before I formed you in the womb, I knew you. Before you were born, I set you apart for my holy purpose. I appointed you to be a prophet to the nations. (Jer. 1:4–5)

It's important to remember that abortion/murder is a forgivable sin. God will forgive you for having an abortion, or for any murder you have committed, if you repent and ask for his forgiveness. And you only need to ask once. A close friend who had an abortion at a young age and later had children confided to me that she has asked God many times to forgive her for having the abortion. As God looks into the heart and sees sincere repentance, he forgives instantly. Ask for God's forgiveness and then accept that Jesus won that forgiveness for you through his death on the cross. Then he rose from the dead and returned to heaven so he could send his Holy Spirit to live and work in you to live a holy life pleasing to him. Once the Holy Spirit comforts you with the knowledge that God has forgiven you, pray that the Holy Spirit will give you the strength to forgive yourself.

War and self–defense

God had never intended for there to be murders in the world. He meant for the world to be a place of peace, love, joy, rest, and security in him. Our sin and rebellion brought all evil into the world, including death, destruction, and murder. This rebellion against God has bred the hatred and evil that lead to war.

Although war is based on hatred and evil, it isn't necessarily considered evil to fight in wars—it depends on whether you're fighting on the side of good or evil. Sometimes good men must fight to stop evil men from pursuing death and destruction. If someone broke into your house, waved a gun around and threatened to kill your family, should you protect yourself and them even if it means having to take the life of the intruder? Of course! We must stand up for the innocent and fight for those who can't defend themselves. If you don't fight, you just become a participant to the evil itself.

It has been suggested that some of the stronger nations of the world should disarm themselves and set an example for other countries. This scenario ignores the fact that not everyone is seeking good. If everyone were seeking good, we wouldn't need a military! In a world of sin, sometimes war is the only way to achieve peace. History has shown that nations that strengthen their militaries are able to maintain peace and prosperity for long periods of time. If a nation isn't adequately defended, evil can easily overtake it. Treaties and alliances can be broken; only strength in military forces can offer the ultimate security.

Jesus said to "turn the other cheek," you might say in your argument that war is always wrong. Through war, someone earned the freedom for you to mention Jesus' name. Jesus did teach that when it comes to our *relationships with people* we shouldn't seek retaliation but should remain at peace with all men. He never, however, said that war was wrong. When he commended a Roman centurion (soldier) for his great faith, he never told him to lay down his sword. (Matt. 8) The Apostle Paul says that one of the roles of government is to punish evil.

Every person should obey the government in power. No government would exist if it hadn't been established by God. The governments which exist have been put in place by God. Therefore, whoever resists the government opposes what God has established. Those who resist will bring punishment on themselves. (Romans 13:1–2)

So going to war isn't a sin but a necessary evil to combat evil. God is not anti-war. He allows it and has even commanded it at times throughout history. War is a sad but legitimate function of human government. So if you're one of many war protesters, please repent of being in rebellion to the authority God has placed over you and of being in rebellion to God. Soldiers who must kill during wartime have not committed murder anymore than the man who defends himself and his family against an intruder. Soldiers are obeying the orders of the government—a government the Bible tells us has been established by God.[6]

Assisted suicide and euthanasia

Assisted suicide is legal in at least one state, but that doesn't make it morally right. God says, "Do not even have murderous thoughts," and when we help someone to end their life, we are committing murder. The only authority God has given human beings to take life is when the state executes a person who is guilty of premeditated murder and other crimes society feels deserve the death penalty. If you'd like God's viewpoint on capital punishment, read the books of Exodus and Leviticus.

We are not to judge the heart; in assisting someone to commit suicide, we may be sending an unrepentant person to hell! If the person has made the Great Exchange, then that person will want God to be in control of when they go home to heaven. God has a purpose for every life he creates, and his purpose for that life is finished when he says it's finished. The same can be said for euthanasia. Even if a person has been in a coma or vegetative state for years, until God calls that person home, he still has a purpose for their life, and he is still able to heal them. We have no right to end that life.

A woman recently made the news when her husband appealed to the courts for the right to allow her to die after a number of years during which she was in a persistent vegetative state. The courts instructed the doctors to remove her feeding tube.[7] While it may not have been God's will that heroic measures were instituted to keep this woman alive in the first place, once those measures are in place, the decision to stop them is certainly questionable. If God had wanted to end the woman's life, he could have done so at any time. The purpose for which he had created her may not have been fulfilled, and who knows if at some point it might have been God's will to heal her.

These cases raise serious moral and ethical questions. Often times this question must be asked before instituting life–extending means: What is the reasonable prognosis? What kind of life will the patient have if life–extending means are used? What if a person has a DNR (Do Not Resuscitate) order? What if a person on life–extending means is declared brain dead?

A pastor friend of mine had to go through that trauma when his wife suffered a massive stroke while at work. She had stopped breathing in the ambulance on the way to the emergency room and was resuscitated by the paramedics. In his case the prognosis by the neuro–surgeon was that her brain was dying. Because she had asked to be an organ donor, her kidneys miraculously matched her son-in-law who was waiting for a kidney transplant half a continent away. Her death meant he is alive and well today.

Every life God has created is precious to him, and he alone knows when there is nothing to be gained by a person's further life on earth. Whether the person has a sound mind or a healthy body are not his criteria for making decisions; his ways are not our ways. He is concerned with each person's eternal destiny.

Why is natural death of a Christian looked upon by so many as a bad thing? The last hymn in The Lutheran Hymnal was *I'm but a Stranger Here, Heaven is my Home.* If, as Paul told the congregation in Philippi, it was far better to leave this earth and be with the Lord, why are so many people afraid of dying? You know, and I do too, that it's because they haven't made the Great Exchange. If you can still read these words and need to make it, what better time is there than right now?

If in your heart you know you need to and are ready to repent of murder in thought or deed, please pray this prayer.

Dear Father, please forgive me for the sin of not respecting life as yours to give and yours alone to take. Forgive me for not respecting all human life you have created. Forgive me for hating (name them here). Please restore all those lives which have been shattered by the murder, including my own. Help me to respect the sanctity of life, including the lives of those people whom I dislike. I accept Jesus as my Lord and Savior and look forward to the day when he will take me to himself to stand with me before your throne in heaven. He will finally return to take me and all believers to heaven to live with you forever in your glorious kingdom. In Jesus' name I pray. Amen.

14

Those Who Practice Magic Arts

People will say to you, "Ask for help from the mediums and the fortunetellers (in Hebrew, those who have familiar spirits)*, who whisper and mutter." Shouldn't people ask their God for help instead? Why should they ask the dead to help the living?* (Is. 8:19)

Those who practice magic arts, be it white or black magic, will not inherit the kingdom of God. Psychics, mediums, fortune tellers, whatever their method, channeling, astrologers, and the like—all are detestable to God. When we consult a psychic for advice about the future, rather than letting God guide and direct our paths, we are in rebellion towards God.

> You must never sacrifice your sons or daughters by burning them alive, practice black magic, be a fortuneteller, witch, or sorcerer, cast spells, ask ghosts or spirits for help, or consult the dead. Whoever does these things is disgusting to the Lord. The Lord your God is forcing these nations out of your way because of their disgusting practices. You must have integrity in dealing with the Lord your God. (Deut. 18:10–13)

Psychics

Psychics are in abundance these days. For several dollars a minute, a telephone psychic will tell you all about your future. I've heard people say, "This psychic has a gift from God. She is so accurate." Don't be fooled! I don't care how good your psychic is, he or she is not 100 percent accurate, and whatever "gift" there may be is definitely not from God.

Most psychics are frauds, but some may in fact get their psychic powers from "familiar spirits." A familiar spirit is one who is familiar with you and your family. Demons are fallen angels; they have been around for thousands of years. When these demon spirits communicate with a medium, they can tell that person a lot about your family members. All demonic spirits have one goal: to stop you from relying upon God and to separate you from God. They are all lying and deceiving spirits. You will never get more than partial truth. God is perfect. He is not right just some of the time. He is right all of the time. If your psychic's "gift" was truly from God, the psychic would *always* be right.

God doesn't give fortune-telling gifts because he wants us to depend on his daily guidance through the Holy Spirit. If he wants to reveal future events, he will do it through his prophetic gifting. A prophet of God will *never* charge money for this gift.

God says we should have no other gods before him. When you consult a psychic, you have put your psychic and his or her predictions ahead of God. God wants us to put all our trust in him. He wants us to tell him of our concerns about the future and to ask for his guidance and direction. We rebel against God by consulting a psychic for answers which are unknowable.

A psychic cannot practice his art without clients. Both psychics *and* those who consult psychics will not inherit the kingdom of God. Everything we ask our psychic we should be asking God instead. Should I marry this person? Should I change jobs? Should I move to a new neighborhood? God is the one with all the answers to our life questions! And with God, you never have to wonder whether the motive for "helping" is money.

> Jesus said, "I'm coming soon! I will bring my reward with me to pay all people based on what they have done. I am the A and the Z, the first and the last, the beginning and the end. Blessed are those who wash their robes so that they may have the right to the tree of life and may go through the gates into the city. Outside are dogs, sorcerers, sexual sinners, murderers, idolaters, and all who lie in what they say and what they do. (Rev. 22:12–15)

All forms of fortune telling are sinful because they seek knowledge of the future apart from that which God chooses to reveal: tarot card readers, palm readers, tea leaf readers, etc.

> "The Lord knows those who belong to him," and "Whoever worships the Lord must give up doing wrong." (2 Tim. 2:19)

Mediums/channelers

People who try to communicate with dead people are wasting their time and angering God. They may be communicating with someone, but it is Satan and the fallen angels who obey him, not God. God doesn't want us to consult with anyone but him for guidance and direction.

A woman recently consulted a medium who, she says, put her in touch with her deceased father, grandmother, uncle, and other relatives. She said, "It couldn't have come from Satan because everything the medium told me was good news, and she knew things about my dad that I haven't told anyone."

Of course it was good news! Satan isn't going to send bad news because then the client wouldn't come back. Surely Satan knows things about her relatives and about her. That's how he puts thoughts in her head which tell her she should consult a medium in the first place! Satan knows a lot about us and about our deceased friends and relatives. He always mixes a little bit of truth in with a truckload of lies.

It wasn't her father or grandmother or uncle this woman was communicating with. It was Satan, the great deceiver and the father of lies. We cannot communicate with the dead, whether they be relatives or "saints" or disciples, or anyone else. This is idolatry.

> Don't turn to psychics or mediums to get help. That will make you unclean. I am the Lord your God. (Lev. 19:31)

King Saul died because he had consulted a medium for guidance instead of putting his trust in God.

> So Saul died because of his unfaithfulness to the Lord: He did not obey the Word of the Lord. He asked a medium to request information from a dead person. He didn't request information form the Lord. So the Lord killed him and turned the kingship over to David, Jesse's son. (1 Chr. 10:13–14)

Whenever *Stella's photograph is taken, a bright, white light appears in the photo, usually over her shoulder. Stella insists that this light is evidence that her deceased sister *Molly is with her. She says she talks to Molly frequently, so it's just natural that Molly would be with her and would appear in pictures with her.

What is really going on with Stella is that she has a familiar spirit attached to her. If she would command it to leave in the name of Jesus, it would go. Stella, however, has welcomed, even invited the familiar spirit to stay by communicating with it, believing it to be her dead sister. Please write these words on your heart: Don't ever try to communicate with your deceased loved ones! If you would just communicate with Jesus, you will see your loved ones again when you die. You can communicate with them then.

The Bible tells us that the dead cannot cross over to be with the living, and the living cannot communicate with the dead. When the rich man wanted Abraham to send Lazarus the beggar, who had died and gone to heaven, to come and help quench his thirst, Abraham told him, "A wide area separates us. People couldn't cross it in either direction even if they wanted to." (Luke 16:26)

Ouija boards are another form of channeling or communicating with the dead which God hates. A Ouija board is not a harmless game! When the cursor moves around the board to spell out names and numbers, who do you think is giving you the answers to your questions? Not God—but Satan! If you have a Ouija board, it is highly recommended that you throw it away, or, even better, burn it. Satan would love for you to keep communicating with him through this "game." Why? The game puts you in rebellion against God by having you consult something other than him for guidance.

> I will condemn people who turn to mediums and psychics and chase after them as though they were prostitutes. I will exclude them from the people. (Lev. 20:6)

We, too, will see eternal death in hell, along with the mediums we consult, if we continue to look to them for answers instead of to God. Why would we go to someone who is trying to play God when we can go directly to God himself?

> Entrust your ways to the Lord. Trust him, and he will act on your behalf. He will make your righteousness shine like a light, your just cause like the noonday sun. (Ps. 37:5–6)

Sorcerers/witches

Sorcerers, witches, warlocks, witch doctors, voodooists, and the like will not inherit the kingdom of God. Sorcerers engage in black magic, using incantations and spells in an effort to harm or murder others. This is not of God; it's Satan's work.

The Wiccan religion claims to practice "white" magic. They say their spells and practices are never used to harm others. The problem with this, however, is that they use spells to benefit themselves rather than depending on God, and their manipulations do affect other people because they change their environment.

One look at the founding of the Wiccan religion in the 1950s by Gerald Gardner (1184–1964), a British civil servant, should tell you this religion is not of God. Gardner was initiated into a witchcraft coven in 1939. He met Aleister Crowley, who founded the Church of Satan, in 1946. Gardner published *Witchcraft Today* in 1954 and *The Meaning of Witchcraft* in 1959.

Gardner considered the occult witchcraft practiced in England to be the remnants of an ancient earth–based worship system. His Wiccan tradition was his attempt to restore that ancient religious system. Gardnerian Wicca was brought to America by Raymond Buckland, whom Gardner met in 1963. Gardnerian Wicca is considered one of the oldest forms of Wicca, and most Wiccans acknowledge it to be the beginning of the Wicca Movement.

Wicca is far removed from Christianity, leaning closer towards Satanism. Gardner was a believer in the power of witchcraft and combined it with some Masonic practices. From his studies in occultism, he also included Tarot cards, wands, chalices, and the pentacle into his practices, along with nudism. Some Gardnerian Wicca innovations have sexual and even bondage–and–discipline overtones. This is not a "harmless" religion you want to get involved with![1]

Witches and warlocks, whether they practice white or black magic, will not enter heaven. Even if a white witch is attempting to heal others with her spells and chants or by placing her hands on someone through Reiki or some other healing method, she is detestable to God because she is not looking to the Triune God as the source for healing. She is practicing idolatry as are those who pay for her services.

There are those who will say, "But it really works. I've seen people who were healed through Reiki." Satan is able to heal people too, but he will grant a temporary healing—just enough to keep the person turning to Reiki and away from God. One person who was healed through Reiki complained that he was healed of his ailment but became plagued with migraine headaches after the healing. This is not a healing that came from God! Reiki is not a harmless therapeutic massage any more than a Ouija board is a harmless board game. Yes, it matters where the source of your healing comes from, whether it comes from heaven or hell.

One Reiki healer insists that everyone who comes to her house and to her healing room tells her how peaceful they feel and how well they sleep that night after their Reiki session. Does this mean the practice is not satanic? Of course not! The devil is able to instill feelings of peace too, but his peace is a temporary peace, which he grants for the sole purpose of separating you from God. Born–again Christians who have entered this same healing room speak of feelings of dread and death, rather than peace. Protected by the full armor of Christ, the devil isn't able to mess with them.

Father Tom Ingoldsby, an Irish priest, said about Reiki, "Opening the door to evil and occult forces will have later side effects. Many people today are falling for Reiki unaware that they are on a dangerous road, as once the door is opened to Satan, it is extremely difficult to get him out. People who go for a Reiki treatment are exposing themselves to occult forces which may give one a false sense of peace of mind or some type of temporary healing. Everyone should be warned that side effects can materialize later." Ingoldsby said former Reiki healers witnessed strange spirits entering them and required deliverance by a priest experienced in exorcisms.[2]

Astrologers

Astrologers guide people in what to do or what not to do at certain times based on the position of the stars and planets at the time of the person's birth. Astrology is another fortune-telling method, and both those who practice and those who rely on its predictions are in rebellion to God.

> Don't let yourselves be tempted to worship and serve what you see in the sky—the sun, the moon, the stars, or anything else. The Lord your God has given them to all people everywhere. (Deut. 4:19)

We are worshiping the heavenly bodies rather than God when we look to them to guide us in our daily living. God wants us to look to him for guidance and direction, not to the daily horoscopes. God gave us our view of the stars as an evidence that he exists. The heavens declare the glory of God.

> This is what the Lord says: Don't learn the practices of the nations. Don't be frightened by the signs in the sky because the nations are frightened by them. (Jer.10:2)

If we get so wrapped up in what our horoscope says each day that we begin to let it control our lives, we cut ourselves off from God's protection. We turn our backs on God, give ourselves over to Satan, and could end up with the same fate as the astrologers.

There are those who say, "Oh, I don't believe what my horoscope says; I just read it for entertainment." Then they find themselves abiding by it anyway. For example, if their horoscope says, "Today isn't a good day to sign any contracts," they may change something they had planned to do to appease the gods or devils of the horoscope. Astrology can be another form of idolatry. If we really want to please God, we will walk away from horoscopes, fortune cookies, etc., and not even read them. Prophesying to the idolatrous nation of Babylon, Isaiah wrote:

> Keep practicing your spells and your evil magic. You have practiced them ever since you were young. You may succeed. You may cause terror. You are worn out by your many plans. Let your astrologers and your stargazers, who foretell the future month by month, come to you, rise up, and save you. They are like straw. Fire burns them. They can't rescue themselves from the flames. There are no glowing coals to keep them warm and no fire for them to sit by. This is how it will be for those who have worked with you, for those who have been with you ever since you were young. They will go their own ways, and there will be no one to save you. (Is. 47:12–15)

Superstitions

We shouldn't let superstitions control us. There is no such thing as luck—good or bad. All good things come from God, and all bad things come from Satan or as a result of man's sinfulness and its corruption of the earth. If we break a mirror, we will not have seven years of bad luck. If we walk under a ladder, we will not have bad luck. If we step on a crack, we will not break our mother's back. If a black cat crosses our path, our lives will be no different than if it had walked around us. If we knock on wood, we will not have good luck. Give up carrying around that rabbit's foot or that St. Anthony medal in your pocket. They do nothing other than weigh you down.

The more confidence we put in a superstition, the more we are turning our backs on God. When we have made the Great Exchange, we trust that God will guide us, care for us, and protect us in any given situation. Following the prediction of a superstition means we are being controlled by fear.

> No fear exists where [God's] love is. Rather, perfect love gets rid of fear, because fear involves punishment. The person who lives in fear doesn't have perfect love. (1 John 4:18)

One of my e-mail friends continuously sends messages to me which end with various superstitions such as, "If you forward this message to seven people in the next five minutes, something wonderful will happen to you at 4 p.m. today," or "If you don't forward this message then something horrible will befall you in the next twenty-four hours." God's blessings come from his goodness—because he loves us—and because they are a result of our obedience to him, not because we did or didn't forward an e-mail.

> These are all the blessings that will come to you and stay close to you because you obey the Lord your God: (Deut. 28:2; *Read this chapter to find out the blessings of obedience and the curses of disobedience.*)

Satan loves these or any other kind of chain letters. If we feel compelled to forward them, then we are obeying the spirit of fear. We are actually placing a curse on our friends when we tell them something bad will happen to them. When I receive these kinds of messages, I immediately delete them and pray for Jesus' atoning blood to remove any curses.

A neighbor believes she must always leave a house or building by the same door through which she entered. When we visit her house and enter through the front door, she is right there when we leave to make sure we don't try to slip out the side door when we leave. "It's bad luck," she insists. This and all superstitions are based on fear, not on faith in God, which is the opposite of fear. You can either allow your life to be controlled by fear or by faith in God, not both.

When we pray to God and know he is controlling all aspects of our lives, we'll be less inclined to believe in coincidences. Is it a coincidence when you pray to God, asking him to relieve your financial burden and then receive an unexpected check in the mail a few days later? Is it fate when you encounter a friend of the opposite sex in the grocery store and rekindle an old romance, or is it God's will at work in your life? We must give thanks and praise to God for all the blessings he bestows on us without ever doubting where they come from.

While writing this book, I had many very clear moments when I knew God wanted me to be writing, when his Holy Spirit was present to work through me to get his Word to others. A couple of times, I ignored his voice and attempted to click on entertaining headlines which were flashing across the top of my computer screen. Whenever I would do this during a period when I knew I was supposed to be writing, the articles wouldn't appear on my screen. It seemed like the computer was taking forever to display them. After waiting for a long period and not having the articles surface, I would return to my writing. Once the thoughts were down on paper, I'd try to retrieve the articles again, and they would appear on my screen within seconds. Coincidence? Not when God is guiding and directing every aspect of my life.

If in your heart you know you need to and are ready to repent of practicing any of the magic arts, having your fortune told, or being superstitious, and you want to receive God's forgiveness, you can say this prayer.

Dear Father, please forgive me for putting my faith in things that you have declared to be evil. You have wisely kept the future hidden so that I may walk by faith and not by sight. In your wisdom you want me to know of your love for me and all human beings. Help me by your Spirit's guiding to take my life one day at a time, forsaking all attempts I've made to see and use demonic powers to my selfish advantage. I know that by Jesus' atoning death on the cross, I have been saved from my sin of trusting in powers you have forbidden. I now declare that Jesus is my Savior and my Lord, and by the power of your Holy Spirit, I will live for Him. I look forward to the day when Jesus will return to take me and all believers to heaven to live with you forever in your glorious kingdom. In Jesus' name I pray. Amen.

15

Those With Selfish Ambitions

But if you are bitterly jealous and filled with self-centered ambition, don't brag. Don't say that you are wise when it isn't true. That kind of wisdom doesn't come from above. It belongs to this world. It is self-centered and demonic. Wherever there is jealousy and rivalry, there is disorder and every kind of evil. (James 3:14–16)

We live in a me, me, me world, putting ourselves above everyone and everything else. If I don't look out for me, who will? Our lives are all too easily about "I want what I want when I want it." Honest people will admit that living this way results in only fleeting glimpses of happiness. God has a better way.

Let's start with the operative Greek words for selfish ambition. *Eri–theia* had a long history in political terms, (i.e. using trickery and illegal acts to put oneself forward as the better/best candidate). It wasn't the ambition to run for or seek office that was selfish, it was the use of illegal, immoral, or unethical means to attain that goal. Unfortunately that aspect isn't heard in the translation "selfish ambition." It's like coveting. All coveting, (i.e. desire to have someone or something), is not sinful. It's sinful only when it takes the breaking of another commandment to obtain. Likewise, it isn't ambition that is selfish. It is the breaking of any other commandments to attain that goal that is condemned. You can and should have ambition. You should want to get an education, learn a trade, be useful as a good steward of the treasury of talents and abilities God has given you.

Unfortunately "selfish ambition" isn't that good of a translation from the original Greek at all. The New English Bible translates selfish ambition as rivalry, and that misses the point too. The root word is *Eris*, the Greek god of discord. The verbal for it is what grammarians call the "middle voice," which doesn't exist in English. From a purely etymological standpoint, the root word for strife or discord is *Eris* within the Body of Christ—the Church purchased with his blood. James Chapter 1 is expanded and emphasized here. The wisdom which is moral, ethical, and legal and does not cause strife is that which builds up the body of

Christ. The self-centered ambition to put oneself forward to be the leader is that "selfish ambition" that is condemned. In other words: You can't truly build up the body of Christ if you are an Elmer Gantry.

For example, the district attorney in Raleigh, NC, was disbarred in June 2007. Judges cited his "selfish" rape prosecution of three Duke University lacrosse players as the reason for his disbarment. Judges said the attorney had been politically motivated when he continued to pursue charges against the young men months after he had reviewed evidence showing them to be innocent.[1]

This man is the perfect example of how self-centered ambition can lead to destruction. His selfishness and desire to be reelected had led him to lie and bear false witness against the lacrosse players, among other sins. In his selfish desire to achieve what he wanted, the attorney had total disregard for the fate and futures of the young men accused of a rape they didn't commit.

Another excellent example of those with selfish ambitions are illegal immigrants. The key word here is *illegal*. Those who sneak into America place their wants and desires ahead of everyone else's. They are attempting to attain something—in this case, United States citizenship—using illegal means and breaking other commandments to do it.

Illegal immigrants selfishly have no regard for those who have been on a waiting list for years trying to enter America legally. Since the United States can only accept and accommodate so many immigrants per year, they are stealing citizenship away from others who are attempting to obtain the status legally. Once in the country, they must lie to just about everyone to keep their status as an illegal alien hidden.

God wants us to welcome strangers and foreigners into our country, but he doesn't expect us to welcome and cater to *illegal* immigrants. They too must obey man's laws and God's laws. If you are an illegal immigrant, you need to repent of stealing and lying. True repentance means you are willing to return to your homeland and attempt to enter America using legal and ethical means. If you have assisted others in trying to enter the country illegally, you too should repent. All of us need to stop voting for politicians who support laws that aid and abet illegal immigrants.

Trusting God

God created us, and he knows we will be happiest when we depend entirely on him to take care of *all* our needs—emotional, spiritual, and physical. So after the Great Exchange is made, we allow him to love and give to the people around us, and we trust him to meet our needs. Everyone who lives this way shares this in common: They are consistently content, peaceful, and joyful. Their motive for acting on behalf of others is pure—it is simply that they trust and desire to please God.

Satan wants to keep us self-focused, including the times when we are *seemingly* unselfish. If we give to the poor by getting rid of junk we don't want lying around the house, or because we want people to see how wonderful we are, or simply to get a deduction on our income tax, then our reasons for giving may very well be purely selfish. Those with selfish ambitions will not receive everlasting life.

> Make no mistake about this: You can never make a fool out of God. Whatever you plant is what you'll harvest. If you plant in the soil of your corrupt nature, you will harvest destruction. But if you plant in the soil of your spiritual nature, you will harvest everlasting life. We can't allow ourselves to get tired of living the right way. Certainly, each of us will receive everlasting life at the proper time if we don't give up. Whenever we have the opportunity, we have to do what is good for everyone, especially for the family of believers. (Gal. 6:7–10)

Kaziah Hancock is a great example of someone whose ambitions are totally unselfish. Hancock began painting portraits of soldiers killed in action and sending the portraits to the soldiers' families. She started with one or two paintings and has now painted over 250 soldiers. Hancock, whose previous paintings had sold for thousands of dollars, refuses to accept any money from the soldiers' families. She has given up thousands of dollars in income to send these young men home to their families, even if only on canvas, after they've been killed.

Rich does not necessarily equal selfish

The Bible is full of warnings to the rich who ignore the poor and exploit people for gain. Now just because someone is rich doesn't automatically mean he has selfish ambitions, but Jesus made it clear that it would be especially hard for the rich to enter the kingdom of heaven. The Great Exchange requires the willingness to lay down everything for Jesus' sake. It is often difficult for the rich to say, "Everything I have and everything I am belong to God, and I will use it all as he directs."

You do not, however, need to be rich to have selfish ambitions. Many people are on welfare who don't need to be. Many have developed a sense of entitlement, an attitude that the government or the world owes them something for nothing. They have selfish ambitions. Those who think of no one outside of themselves or their immediate family have selfish ambitions. They are not capable of loving others as God has commanded us to do. They are too busy loving themselves. They go after things, money, status, or position, thinking these will bring happiness, often at the expense of others. Many celebrities, including Cheryl Ladd, Gary Busey, Chad Everett, Randy Travis, and Tiny Lister, to name just a few, will tell you that getting all the world has to offer does *not* fill the empty space.

> Don't love the world and what it offers. Those who love the world don't have the Father's love in them. Not everything that the world offers—physical gratification, greed, and extravagant lifestyles—comes from the Father. It comes from the world, and the world and its evil desires are passing away. But the person who does what God wants lives forever. (1 John 2:15–17)

We cannot please God when we are selfish, because it is his character to give. Since he has given so much to us, including his Son, he wants us to give generously to others. People who give for the sheer joy of giving tend to be happy people!

> All goes well for the person who is generous and lends willingly. He earns an honest living. (Ps. 112:5)

> Whoever is generous will be blessed because he has shared his food with the poor. (Prov. 22:9)

> Tell them to do good, to do a lot of good things, to be generous, and to share. (1 Tim. 6:18)

We have selfish ambitions, too, when we withhold our tithes from God. Of whom are we thinking when we refuse to tithe, or when we fail to give when we see a need? Why, ourselves, of course—certainly not God or our brothers and sisters in Christ. God tells us not to store up treasures on earth, but to store up treasures in heaven. Refusing to honor God in tithing and giving is selfish.

> Now, the effects of the corrupt nature are obvious ... selfish ambitions ... and things like that. I've told you in the past and I'm telling you again that people who do things like that will not inherit the kingdom of God. (Gal. 5:19–21)

Other acts of selfishness

Everything we do should be done for the glory of God. If my motives for writing this book are selfish ones, to try to achieve fame or fortune, then I am guilty of having selfish ambitions and will not inherit the kingdom of heaven.

> If the Lord does not build the house, it is useless for the builders to work on it. If the Lord does not protect a city, it is useless for the guard to stay alert. (Ps. 127:1)

Unless the Lord writes the book, it is useless for the author to work on it. If I allow the Holy Spirit to help with the writing of this book and my motives for writing it are not selfish, then I bring glory to the Lord. My motive for writing this particular book is to see readers turn away from sins that bring eternal death and to receive the Great Exchange of Jesus' life for their own, so they can inherit the kingdom of God. God is glorified, and I am blessed.

People with selfish ambitions are everywhere. A couple attended an auction at the church they belonged to for a short time before joining their present congregation. A silent auction was held in which items were placed on tables and anyone who wanted the item needed to write a bid at least one dollar higher than the last. When the host announced bidding was over, kids helping at the auction scrambled to collect all the pencils and stretch a rope across the items so people wouldn't continue to bid after the time for bidding had ended.

The auction was a church function; most of those present were members of the congregation. Having kids gather pencils and close off the bidding area shouldn't have been necessary! The necessity of "security" at the auction became clear to this couple when they paid for their items at the end of the auction. A relative who attended with them had been the high bidder on a large item, but when she went to pay for it at the auction's close, she learned someone had snuck in a bid after the host had announced the bidding closed. Someone had "stolen" the item from her.

Now this was supposed to be a fund-raising event for a *church*, hosted by *Christians*, and presumably supported by *people who care about God's work*. Do you think God was honored by this? What did he see when he looked into the hearts of the people who were there? What is the eternal price tag for that item won by cheating because the person had selfish ambitions? Without repentance—a true change of heart—the cost may be heaven itself.

In contrast, the couple attended the silent auction this year for the church they now attend, and there were no pencil collectors or "security" to ensure no one would try to sneak bids in after closing time. People's hearts at this church are different. These Christians are a living body of Christ with most members doing their best to walk as Jesus did. Selfish ambitions didn't spoil this auction.

Selfishness is built in

Human beings are by nature selfish; we have to be taught to consider others before ourselves. Most Christian parents try to teach their children to put God first and others next. When other parents don't try to teach the same values and traits to their children, it makes it difficult to help your own children to become less selfish.

> These are the commands ... the Lord your God commanded me to teach you ... Repeat them to your children. Talk about them when you're at home or away, when you lie down or get up. (Deut. 6:1–7)

A couple and their young children used to join another couple and their teenage children for dinner in various restaurants around town and would always split the tab. It didn't bother them that their children were eating at kids' meal prices and their friends' children at adult prices. What bothered them was the selfishness of the teenage son. No matter what restaurant they dined at, he would always order the most expensive item on the menu, yet his parents never reprimanded him for it. In fact, they even joked about it! It was selfish behavior on the son's part, but it was the responsibility of his parents to correct him.

The parents were unwilling or unable to correct the teenager, and it is very likely he was modeling their behavior. On the few nights the adults dined without the kids present, the father would snatch the bill when it arrived, add up the amounts of his items, and hand the couple the bill along with his portion of the tab. The couple would then have to pay their portion, plus the tax on all the items, plus the tip. Needless to say, they seldom dine out with this couple anymore simply because they abhor their selfishness. Perhaps they should have asked for separate checks. That may very well have headed off the problem and saved a friendship.

God wants us to teach and model to our children his character—love, faithfulness, goodness, selflessness. As they grow up, they are to transfer their dependence from us, the parents, to God to direct their lives. There is no faith in selfishness, and so there can be no eternal life in heaven for those ruled by selfish ambition. The fate of those who do not honor God and mistreat their children by not teaching them his ways is not pretty.

For example, parents who park in disabled parking spaces when they have no disability are teaching their children selfishness. Parents who tell their children to lie about their ages when seeking to pay less for theater tickets, amusement park tickets, or dinners are teaching their children not only to have selfish ambitions, but to lie and steal as well. We are to be an example of unselfishness to our children as we help them to grow in faith in the Lord.

> How horrible it will be for the world because it causes people to lose their faith. Situations that cause people to lose their faith will arise. How horrible it will be for the person who causes someone to lose his faith! (Matthew 18:7)

If in your heart you know you need to and are ready to repent of selfishness, and you want to receive God's forgiveness, you can say this prayer.

Dear Father, please forgive me for being selfish. Forgive me for not putting you first, others next, and myself last, trusting you to look out for me and to bless me. Help me to always consider my ambitions and motives before acting in the future, so I can act from a clean heart and glorify you. I accept Jesus as my Lord and Savior, and I know he has cleansed me from the sin of selfishness and all my sins. I look forward to the day when he will return to take me and all believers to heaven to live with you forever in your glorious kingdom. In Jesus' name I pray. Amen.

16

The Sexually Immoral

It is God's will that you keep away from sexual sin as a mark of your devotion to him. Each of you should know that finding a husband or wife for yourself is to be done in a holy and honorable way, not in the passionate, lustful way of people who don't know God. (1 Thess. 4:3–5)

There are so many different kinds of sexual sins and the Bible has so much to say about sexual immorality, whole books have been written on sexual sins alone. I have covered the sexual sins of adultery and homosexuality in separate chapters because they are mentioned specifically and separately in the Bible as sins which are punishable by eternal damnation in hell. However, the Bible tells us that no sexually immoral people will inherit the kingdom of heaven.

> We shouldn't sin sexually as some of them did. Twenty-three thousand of them died on one day. (1 Cor. 10:8)

Let me reiterate from a previous chapter that having sex outside of marriage is sinful. People who do not repent of this sin and accept Jesus as their Lord and Savior will suffer horrible consequences. In our culture today, many people, including some who call themselves Christians, have decided that many things the Bible calls sin are actually okay to do. However, a human being's opinion doesn't change God or his Word.

> The acts of the sinful nature are obvious: illicit sex, perversion, promiscuity … orgies and the like. I've told you in the past and I'm telling you again that people who do things like that will not inherit the kingdom of God. (Gal. 5:19–21)

Bestiality

Having sex with animals is about as low as one can go in being sexually immoral, and it is extremely dangerous spiritually. Remember, you become one with what you have sex with. To take the spirit of an animal as part of yourself is to make yourself less than truly human. You need to repent and let Jesus restore you to spiritual health.

> A man who has sexual intercourse with an animal must be put to death. You must kill the animal, too. When a woman offers herself sexually to any animal, you must kill both the woman and the animal. They must be put to death. They deserve to die. (Lev. 20:15–16)

God considered bestiality so dangerous to the spiritual and physical condition of people and animals that he ordered both the offender and the animal victim to be put to death. The reason for this was so the defilement could not be passed on to offspring of the human or the animal and corrupt future generations. Thanks to the blood sacrifice of Jesus, those who have had sex with animals can be forgiven and restored if they repent and ask for God's forgiveness won through Jesus' death.

Child molestation

One of every five children will be molested during their childhood. In the majority of cases, the perpetrator is a relative, close friend of the family, or someone the child knows and trusts. Child molestation knows no boundaries. It happens as often in middle class and upper–middle class families as well as in poorer families.[1]

Child molestation does not just mean sexual intercourse. It includes any kind of sexual touching or exhibitionism. Child molesters know what they are doing is sexually immoral. That's why they always try to get the child off by themselves and commit their disgusting acts in private. A child molester can also be another child, usually one who has been molested himself. It is not uncommon to hear about a twelve year old molesting a six year old. A child molester is anyone who engages in any kind of sexual activity with a child.

> Even a child makes himself known by his actions, whether his deeds are pure or right. (Prov. 20:11)

> And whoever welcomes a child like this in my name welcomes me. These little ones believe in me. It would be best for the person who causes one of them to lose faith to be drowned in the sea with a large stone hung around his neck. (Matt. 18:5–6)

> So if your hand causes you to lose your faith, cut it off! It is better for you to enter life disabled than to have two hands and go to hell, to the fire that cannot be put out. If your foot causes you to lose faith, cut if off! It is better for you to enter life lame than to have two feet and be thrown into hell. If your eye causes you to lose your faith, tear it out! It is better for you to enter the kingdom of God with one eye than to have two eyes and be thrown into hell. In hell worms that eat the body never die, and the fire is never put out. (Mark 9:43–48)

It is generally thought that child molesters, once caught and convicted, should not be allowed back into society, that they cannot be rehabilitated. There is hope for them, however, through Jesus Christ, who can and will cleanse the child molester from all unrighteousness. The Holy Spirit will change his heart and change his eternal destiny. The child molester who makes the Great Exchange has won salvation through Jesus Christ just as any sinner who repents. Christ will remove the feelings of lust for children that torment the molester and often contribute to the corruption of the child's personality as well. The Great Exchange will allow a restoration of sanity.

> God is faithful and reliable. If we confess our sins, he forgives them and cleanses us from everything we've done wrong. If we say, "We have never sinned," we turn God into a liar and his Word is not in us. (1 John 1:9–10)

Frigidity

Frigidity is probably the last thing people think of when they think of sexual immorality, but since it falls outside God's plan for married couples to experience true intimacy, it needs to be dealt with. Frigidity is usually associated with women, although men, too, can be guilty of the sin. Sometimes considered a nervous or psychological disorder, as well as a sin, frigidity occurs when one partner doesn't want to have sex with their spouse and sometimes doesn't even want to be touched by their partner. It often occurs in those who have been sexually molested, and it is all too common in those women who have been prostitutes. It is even reported in women and men who have grown up with a stern, unaffectionate father.

Whatever the underlying reason, one partner has an aversion to having sex with his or her spouse. Frigidity is not of God; it is a manifestation of Satan at work. He tries to entice us to disobey God's commands and keep us from having healthy relationships however he can.

> Husbands and wives should satisfy each other's sexual needs. A wife doesn't have authority over her own body, but her husband does. In the same way, a husband doesn't have authority over his own body, but his wife does. Don't withhold yourselves from each other unless you agree to do so for a set time to devote yourselves to prayer. Then you should get back together so that Satan doesn't use your lack of self-control to tempt you. (1 Cor. 7:3–5)

Frigidity in one partner can tempt or lead to other sexual sins committed by their spouse, such as adultery or incest. It is also responsible for many divorces. Frigidity does not belong in a Christian marriage, and those who are frigid need to repent and be healed, delivered, and set free by the power of Jesus' death and resurrection.

Why not take the time to read the Song of Solomon. This book of the Bible shows that God's creation of sexual desire and passion is a part of his good creation. It might even help if the husband read aloud the part of the bridegroom and the wife read aloud the part of the bride.

Incest

When we think of the sin of incest, we often think of sex between a parent and child or between siblings, but incest includes sexual relations between any family members who are not husband and wife.

> Never have sexual intercourse with your mother. She is your own mother. Never have sexual intercourse with her.

> Never have sexual intercourse with your stepmother. She is related to you through your father.

> Never have sexual intercourse with your stepsister, whether she is your father's daughter or your mother's daughter. It makes no difference whether or not she was born in your house.

> Never have sexual intercourse with your granddaughter, whether she is your son's daughter or your daughter's daughter, because she is related to you.

Never have sexual intercourse with a daughter of your father and his wife. She is your own sister.

Never have sexual intercourse with your father's sister. She is your paternal aunt.

Never have sexual intercourse with your mother's sister. She is your maternal aunt.

Never have sexual intercourse with the wife of your father's brother. She, too, is your aunt.

Never have sexual intercourse with your daughter–in–law. She is your son's wife.

Never have sexual intercourse with a woman and her daughter or a woman and her granddaughter. They are related. Doing this is perverted.

While your wife is living, never marry her sister as a rival wife and have sexual intercourse with her. (Lev. 18:7–18)

Pornography

Viewing pornography is an addiction to lust which has been proven to lead to sexual crimes and murder. It also leads to frigidity towards one's spouse and is extremely destructive to the healthy intimacy of a marriage.[2] Serial rapists and murderers Ted Bundy and Gary Ridgway both blame pornography for inciting their crimes. Bundy began viewing pornography as an adolescent. Ridgway used the pornography to fuel his passion for sex and murder before killing his victims.[3] Pornography can create a desire to rape in men who never possessed this desire before, and it can increase the desire to rape in men who previously had the desire to rape.[4]

A sixteen–year–old boy would repeatedly view pornographic movies while baby–sitting his niece and nephew. His aunt and uncle learned of his addiction when they received their cable bill and realized the young man had been purchasing the movies and viewing them in the company of their young children. They informed the boy's parents, who reimbursed their in–laws for the movies, but their response was, "Oh well, boys will be boys."

Yes, boys will be boys. Christian boys will be boys who obey the Word of God, and boys who *say* they are Christians but aren't will continue to view pornography because they haven't made the Great Exchange. My guess is that this young man, now twenty-three years old, is struggling with an addiction to pornography that is interfering with his relationships with women. I wonder if the parents' attitude would have been different had they been told their son had been viewing homosexual movies. Somehow I believe this may have caused them to worry about their son's eternal soul, but whether the movies were homosexual or heterosexual doesn't matter; the eternal consequences for immoral sexual behavior are the same.

Viewing pornography has escalated in the past few years due to easy Internet access and to the increase in the number of pornographic sites. Sex is the number one topic searched on the Internet. Some estimates suggest that nearly 72 million people visit one or more of the over 4 million Internet pornography sites per year.[5] Christians, including clergy, are not immune to pornography addiction. The rates of addiction have increased in the Christian community over the past few years to a level where they are almost as high as pornography addiction rates among non-Christians.[6]

Citizens for Community Values in Ohio recently proposed legislation that would make it a crime for convicted sex offenders to purchase or possess pornography. The correlation between pornography and sex crimes is so high that the organization is attempting to lower the number of sex crimes committed by eliminating just one factor: pornography. Hopefully the idea will spread to other states.[7]

Nothing good has ever come from pornography, and viewing it—especially at an early age—is, at the very least, destructive to relationships. As other human beings and the sex act (which God created to be an expression of love), become objectified, violent behavior has been shown to develop. The same can be said of listening to certain genres of music. Rap and Hip Hop and the general themes of degrading women can develop into the listener regarding women as objects to be used and abused.

Hope for breaking the addiction to pornography lies in Jesus Christ. God's Holy Spirit can and will deliver you from the bondage of pornography addiction if you'll call on the Lord for deliverance and use the means available to help you. The Holy Spirit will remove the sexual lust associated with viewing pornography, will cleanse you, and will set you free.

Prostitution

Because God created sex to be an expression of love and to be the way children are created, all within the context of a marriage and family, he hates prostitution. Male and female prostitutes will not enter the kingdom of heaven, and neither will the men and women who pay for the services of prostitutes. Prostitutes don't understand this, thinking, "My body is mine. What right does anyone have to tell me what I can do with it?" People who solicit prostitutes think, "He/she wants the money; I'm not hurting anyone. This is consensual sex." But God knows that all involved are degraded and debased by prostitution.

When you have sex with someone, you become "one flesh" with that person. When you have sex with a prostitute, you are having sex with her and with everyone else she has ever had sex with. The possibility of true intimacy with just one person—your mate—just as with pornography, is seriously damaged. Your immortal soul is torn in so many different fragments that only Jesus Christ can put it back together again.

Another reason God has prohibited prostitution is because he knows sexual promiscuity promotes physical illnesses. Sexually transmitted diseases are just one physical consequence of casual sex with multiple partners; some other physical effects include depression and the development of some forms of cancer.

> However, the body is not for sexual sin but for the Lord, and the Lord is for the body. God raised the Lord, and by his power God will also raise us. Don't you realize that your bodies are parts of Christ's body? Should I take the parts of Christ's body and make them parts of a prostitute's body? That's unthinkable! Don't you realize that the person who unites himself with a prostitute becomes one body with her? God says, "The two will be one." However, the person who unites himself with the Lord becomes one spirit with him. (1 Cor. 6:13–17)

> Stay away from sexual sins. Other sins that people commit don't affect their bodies the same way sexual sins do. People who sin sexually sin against their own bodies. Don't you know that your body is a temple that belongs to the Holy Spirit? The Holy Spirit, whom you received from God, lives in you. You don't belong to yourselves. You were bought for a price. So bring glory to God in the way you use your body. (1 Cor. 6:18–20)

> Don't you know that wicked people won't inherit the kingdom of God? Stop deceiving yourselves! People who continue to commit sexual sins, who worship false gods, those who commit adultery, homosexuals, or thieves, those who are greedy or drunk, who use abusive language, or who rob people will not inherit the kingdom of God. That's what some of you were! But you have been washed and made holy, and you have received God's approval in the name of the Lord Jesus Christ and in the Spirit of our God. (1 Cor. 6:9–11)

> The sexually immoral will find themselves in the fiery lake of burning sulfur. (Rev. 21:8)

Sexual lust

Adultery, fornication, incest, bestiality and the like—all begin with lust. Sexual lust is sin of the mind and heart, rather than the body.

> Jesus said, "You have heard that it was said, 'Never commit adultery.' But I can guarantee that whoever looks at a woman and desires her has already committed adultery in his heart. (Matt: 5:27–28)

Masturbation may also be a sin of lust. Those who masturbate abuse their bodies and fornicate or commit adultery in their minds and hearts.

> The human mind is the most deceitful of all things. It is incurable. No one can understand how deceitful it is. I, the Lord, search minds and test hearts. I will reward each person for what he has done. I will reward him for the results of his actions. (Jer. 17:9–10)

Lust taken to the extreme can be found in nymphomania (females with excessive or abnormal sexual cravings) and satyrism (males with excessive or abnormal sexual cravings). With a problem that appears to be the opposite of frigidity, but which often comes from the same sources, those who have nymphomania or satyrism cannot get enough sex. They fantasize about it constantly and partake of sex anywhere and any way they can. This is Satan at work again. Many serial killers suffer from satyrism.

One look or one thought is not lust, but a second look or thought or a third, fourth, or more will develop into lust. God is ready to forgive your sin of lust if you will repent and ask his forgiveness.

Final note

This list of sexually immoral sins is not exhaustive; for instance, I did not include the deadly sins of debauchery or orgies, even though they are listed in the Bible as damnable sins. (Rom. 13:13, Gal. 5:21, 1 Pet. 4:3) Obviously if you are involved in debauchery or orgies, you are already committing fornication and/or adultery. Just know that *any* kind of sexual activity which is not focused in a loving way on your spouse is contrary to God's will.

Remember, God invented sex, and he did it for our enjoyment and for procreation of the human race. God knows that true enjoyment of sex—as opposed to the sinful use of sex, which always eventually leads us into bondage and to a place of heart emptiness—can only be had in a faithful, loving, secure marriage.

If you are ready to repent of sexual immorality and receive forgiveness so that your name can be written in the Lamb's book of life, you can say this prayer.

Dear Father, please forgive me for my sexual sins. I realize that I have harmed myself and others by these acts and thoughts that are directly contrary to your holy will. I ask you to forgive me and bless and heal me and those whom I have hurt. I ask you to help me to remain pure as I begin my Christian walk. I accept Jesus as my Lord and Savior and know that his blood shed on the cross has cleansed me from the deserved punishment for all sexual impurity and unrighteousness. I look forward to the day when Jesus will return and take me and all believers to heaven to live with you forever in your glorious kingdom. In Jesus' name I pray. Amen.

Those who would like more information about deliverance from sexual sin or pornography addiction can contact the following organizations:

Pure Life Ministries
14 School Street
Dry Ridge, KY 41035
(859) 824-4444
www.purelifeministries.org

Pure Life Ministries offers a six- to twelve-month live-in recovery program for those struggling with sexual sin or pornography addictions.

Faithful and True Ministries
15798 Venture Lange
Eden Prairie, MN 55344
www.faithfulandtrueministries.org

Faithful and True Ministries offers five-day intensive workshops for those struggling with sexual addictions.

17

The Thieves

Thieves must quit stealing and, instead, they must work hard. They should do something good with their hands so that they'll have something to share with those in need. (Eph. 4:28)

God's character is love—acting on *behalf* of others, not against them. If you take something that doesn't belong to you, you are breaking one of his commandments. He clearly states, "Never steal," (Ex. 20:15) and tells us what will happen if we do: "Thieves and those who rob people will not inherit the kingdom of God." (1 Cor. 6:10) God wants us to bless people, not deceive or exploit them.

It may come as a surprise to communists and socialists who seem to believe that everything belongs to the state and nothing belongs to individuals, but God establishes and approves of the ownership of private property. You might take the time to read the confrontation between the prophet Nathan and King David in 2 Samuel 12. It is very enlightening.

Everyone knows what a thief is. I don't think I need to go into great detail describing one. It is someone who takes something that doesn't belong to him. If you walk into a store and take something without paying for it, you're a thief. If you break into someone's home and take some of their possessions, you're a burglar and a thief. If you take home a pencil from work, you're a thief. If you are given too much change at the store and don't return the overage, you're a thief.

A friend used to be a school teacher. It was often very rewarding when the class was filled with students willing to study and learn. Every now and then a bad apple in the class tried to spoil the whole class with disruptive antics that stole both time and the opportunity to learn from all the rest of the students. Yes, disruptive behavior is also a very persuasive form of stealing.

A swindler is a tricky thief. He doesn't directly take something that doesn't belong to someone and walk away with it. He does it in a more round-about way, attempting to cheat his neighbor out of something. A swindler cheats on his taxes. He marries several different women for the sole purpose of draining their bank accounts. He entices the elderly to invest in his nonexistent business. He coaxes people into pyramid schemes. He cons someone into giving him their credit card number and uses it to rack up debts on the person's account. He might even be the head of a large corporation like Enron, taking literally millions of dollars in a swindle. A thief by any other name is still a thief.

Child abductors and kidnappers

Those who abduct infants or children are the most disgusting kind of thieves because they are stealing *someone* rather than *something*. Over the past several years, several women have faked pregnancies and then have attempted to steal other women's newborn babies. As I write this, an 11-day old baby girl has just been recovered in Lonedell, Missouri, after a woman broke into a home, slashed the mother's throat, and stole her baby.[1]

Stealing infants usually is accompanied by a host of sins—months of lying to family, friends, neighbors, and coworkers, assault, and even murder—all to achieve the sin of stealing someone who belongs to someone else. Just in case you weren't up on this, lying is also stealing the truth from those who would act differently if they knew the truth.

Those who abduct children and adolescents are guilty of the same and usually worse. Many child abductions are the result of lust, leading to sexual abuse of the child. Infant and child abductors cannot enter the kingdom of heaven unless they repent of their thoughts and actions, change their attitude and behavior, and make the Great Exchange.

A couple from New Jersey kidnapped their own nineteen-year-old daughter, bound and gagged her, placed her in their car, and attempted to drive her to another state where they planned to force her to have an abortion. The woman was able to escape and contact police, and the parents were sent to jail. An adult child no longer belongs to anyone but God, but these parents are as guilty of kidnapping as they would have been had they stolen someone else's child. The fact that they planned to force their daughter to murder her unborn child just adds to their sins. Thank God that they, too, can repent and be forgiven thanks to Jesus' atoning death on the cross.[2]

Jesus died for all sinners, including serial killers and rapists, child abductors and molesters, and those who try to cause others to sin—in other words, all of us. We all have the opportunity to repent, to be forgiven, and to exchange our lives for Christ's life in us.

Stealing tithes and offerings

We are thieves when we withhold our tithes and offerings from God.

> Can a person cheat God? Yet, you are cheating me! But you ask, 'How are we cheating you?' When you don't bring a tenth of your income and other contributions. So a curse is on you because the whole nation is cheating me! Bring one-tenth of your income into the storehouse so that there my be food in my house. Test me in this way, says the Lord of Armies. See if I won't open the windows of heaven for you and flood you with blessings. Then, for your sake, I will stop insects from eating your crops. They will not destroy the produce of your land. The vines in your field will not lose their unripened grapes, says the Lord of Armies. All nations will call you blessed because you will be a delightful land, says the Lord of Armies. (Mal. 3:8–10)

Many who call themselves Christians don't tithe, usually citing the fact that tithing is mentioned in the Old Testament but not in the New Testament. Therefore the reasoning of the selfish sinful flesh says that since Jesus obeyed all the laws of the Old Testament, we, living in New Testament times, don't have to give 10 percent of our income to the Lord for the work of his Church.

Tithing won't get you into heaven as a work. Jesus' blood is the only atonement for sin. However, his redeeming work includes changing lives and changing hearts. Jesus said: "If you love Me, you'll do what I say." (John 14:15) 1 John 3:9 says, "The one who is born of God does not continue to sin." To sin is to not obey what Jesus says to do with your heart and with your words and with your deeds. Jesus said, "Love the Lord your God with all your heart and all your mind and all your strength." What does that mean? It means with everything you've got in you, love—act on behalf of and obey—the Lord. Once the Holy Spirit enlightens your heart and mind, you'll know that everything belongs to God and has only been entrusted to us as stewards.

The tithe, 10 percent of what God entrusts to us, already belongs to God. He can reclaim it all at any time. What he does do is ask for the tithe and then offerings (giving) as he directs. All this is to be done cheerfully. Where does the cheer come from? It comes from loving and trusting God! It comes from knowing God loves you and isn't just waiting for an excuse to smack you around but rather is trying to get you to come under the place of protection and into the shower of blessing.

Jesus applauded the widow in the temple who came in, and out of her need, trusting God to give her a harvest on what she sowed, gave everything she had. God wants us to bring the tithe, not because we "have" to, but because we love and trust him and desire to obey him. (This is the work of the Holy Spirit.) People who withhold the tithe (once they know the truth as opposed to those who don't know any better), giving whatever excuses, including theological ones, are people who don't entirely trust God. They feel a need to or just want to hold on to "their" money. They seek God's hand to fix their problems instead of seeking his face to know him better and to become like him. On the last day, he will say he doesn't know us if our hearts do not entirely belong to him. A "me first" self-centeredness in refusing to give God the first 10 percent is a symptom that our hearts do not entirely belong to him. If we perceive then that our hearts do not entirely belong to him, the solution is for us to repent and call on him to change our hearts—that is the Holy Spirit's job—and he will answer that prayer with a *yes!*

Jesus fulfilled all the law, that is true, but he did it so that through his redemptive work, we could too. Jesus did not abolish the law, and we, too, are expected to obey all of God's commandments to the best of our ability, even if not perfectly. If we are surrendered totally to Jesus and we are living after the Spirit and not the flesh, then we will obey his commandments, and we'll do it with peace and joy.

The problem is simply stated: We need to get cause and effect straight. Heaven is not the result of tithing any more than it is the result of any other good deed. Tithing does not cause us to go to heaven. Tithing, along with other even more important things (see Matt. 23:23–34), is a sign of the state of the heart which is brought about when a person is truly born again. Jesus said, "Unless you be born again, you cannot enter the kingdom of heaven." (John 3:3) So we focus on Jesus, yearning to be more like him, longing to serve him, and desiring to show all the fruit of the Spirit abundantly in our lives. We desire two things more than any others: his soon appearing, and, on that day, hearing him say, "Well done, you good and faithful servant."

What you really need to take from this is that your money isn't really *yours*. When you've made the Great Exchange, you'll realize that everything you have belongs to God. When you don't tithe, you're wanting to hang onto *your* money. It isn't yours! You can spend that 10 percent wherever you like, but you must remember that it isn't your money you're spending; it's God's! If you are only giving 2 or 3 percent or less to God when he has asked for and expects 10 percent, then he considers that you're giving the other 7 or 8 percent to the devil. That money is not going to be blessed. God won't shower you with financial blessings when you're stealing money from him and giving it to Satan, which is what you're doing when you don't hand it over to God.

A couple married ten years began tithing in September 2005. They had always wanted to tithe but thought they couldn't afford to. By the time they made the mortgage payment, purchased the kids' homeschool curriculums and paid fees for outside activities, then paid for utilities, food, and all the other expenses of daily living, the paycheck was spent and they were broke until the next payday. Since they began to tithe, God has poured down the blessings on them. They've been able to pay all the bills plus have a little left over for entertainment. The tithe is always the first thing to come out of the check each week, not the last. They now view tithing as God giving them 90 percent rather than them giving him 10 percent.

The bottom line is that you cannot serve two masters. You can't serve both God and money. If you aren't tithing, Jesus very well may say to you on judgment day, "I know where your heart is. You treasure money more than me. I don't know you, you thief."

If you are ready to turn from being a thief and receive forgiveness through Jesus' shed blood, you can say this prayer.

Dear Father, please forgive me for harming others by stealing. Every time I stole I showed I didn't trust you enough to give me all that I needed for this body and life. Forgive me too for not trusting you enough to give you what is yours. Everything I have, I have because of you. Everything I am and have belongs to you as my Creator and Redeemer. I pledge today to obey your commandment to not steal, including stealing your tithes. I accept Jesus as my Lord and Savior and look forward to the day when he will return to take me and all believers to heaven to live with you forever. In Jesus' name I pray. Amen.

18

The Unbelievers

God loved the world this way: He gave his only Son so that everyone who believes in him will not die but will have eternal life. God sent his Son into the world, not to condemn the world, but to save the world. Those who believe in him won't be condemned. But those who don't believe are already condemned because they don't believe in God's only Son. (John 3:16–18)

Believing in a God you can't see requires faith. To illustrate this, I'll share an old joke with you. A first–grade teacher was trying to explain evolution to her class. She asked one of the students, "Do you see the tree outside?"

"Yes" the child responded.

"And do you see the grass outside?"

"Yes," he answered again.

"And do you see the sky?" the teacher asked.

"Yes, I see the sky."

"And do you see God?"

"No," answered the child.

"That's my point," the teacher said. "We can't see God because he isn't there. He doesn't exist."

Another child asked the teacher if she, too, could ask some questions of the boy. The teacher agreed she could.

"Do you see the tree outside?" she asked her classmate.

"Yes," the boy answered.

"Do you see the grass outside?"

"Yes."

"Do you see the sky?"

"Yes."

"Do you see the teacher?" she asked.

"Yes."

"Do you see her brain?"

"No," he replied.

"Then according to the lesson she just taught us herself, she doesn't have one," the girl said. "It doesn't exist because we can't see it."

> Indeed our lives are guided by faith, not by sight. (2 Cor. 5:7)

Believing through faith

A Harris poll taken in October 2006 found that 42 percent of adults aren't absolutely certain there's a God, up from 34 percent taken three years earlier.[1] Almost half the adult population doesn't know or believe in God the Father of Jesus. Forget all the other chapters of this book for a minute. Although buried at the end of the book, this chapter is the most important. If you don't know Jesus, it doesn't matter whether or not you overcome the other sins mentioned thus far. How can you plan to go to heaven to live eternally with a God you're not sure even exists?

Faith is seeing the invisible and believing the impossible, and it is *behaving* as though what you *say you believe is actually true.* When Jesus appeared to his disciples after having risen from the dead, Thomas wasn't with them. They told Thomas when he returned, "We have seen the Lord." Thomas said, "Unless I see the nail marks in his hands and put my fingers where the nails were and put my hand into his side, I won't believe it."

A week later, Jesus appeared to his disciples again, and this time Thomas was with them. This time Thomas believed. Jesus said to Thomas, "You believe because you've seen me. Blessed are those who haven't seen me but believe." (John 20:29) Stop doubting and believe! Jesus is alive and well. You *must* believe in him or you won't be spending eternity in heaven with him.

What does it mean to "believe in him"? Well, it *doesn't* mean that you simply *say* you believe. Even the devil and his angels believe in God. We'll grant here that the devil and his legions have no choice but to believe that God is. After all, God drove them out of heaven into the abyss. How could they not believe?

> You believe that there is one God. That's fine! The demons also believe that, and they tremble with fear. (James 2:19)

The Holy Spirit has made you spiritually alive. Faith, trust, and belief in the Triune God is a gift and a miracle. You were by nature dead in your trespasses and sins. Now alive in the Spirit, born anew or from above, you are able to make the Great Exchange. You live by *his* faith and by *his* power. All "good works" and all resisting the temptation to sin come from *his* life in us.

Salvation is simple: Believe in the Lord Jesus Christ, and you will be saved. You don't get to heaven by being a "good person" or by doing good works, because no one is good enough to stand in the presence of God, who is holy. When we come to know we are sinners in need of a Savior, and we repent of our sins and by the power of the Holy Spirit in us, accept Jesus' atoning blood to cover our sins, we receive forgiveness from God. In making Jesus Lord of our lives, we enter into the kingdom of heaven. Our lives are different when we call Jesus Lord, as he rules and directs through the power of the Holy Spirit.

> By believing you receive God's approval, and by declaring your faith you are saved. (Rom. 10:9)

> God saved you through faith as an act of kindness. You had nothing to do with it. Being saved is a gift from God. It's not the result of anything you've done, so no one can brag about it. (Eph. 2:8–9)

> Jesus said, "Not everyone who says to me, 'Lord, Lord!' will enter the kingdom of heaven, but only the person who does what my Father in heaven wants. Many will say to me on that day, 'Lord, Lord, didn't we prophesy in your name? Didn't we force out demons and do many miracles by the power and authority of your name?' Then I will tell them publicly, 'I've never known you. Get away from me, you evil people.'" (Matt. 7:21)

Jesus is Lord!

When you read for yourself Jesus' words in the New Testament (words he spoke in person while on earth are found in Matthew, Mark, Luke, and John; words he spoke in person after his resurrection are found in the Acts of the Apostles and the Revelation to John), you can only come to one of three conclusions: Jesus is a liar, Jesus is crazy, or Jesus is Lord of all and the King who will return to gather his own into heaven.

So what is the evidence which helps us decide? Jesus' miracles were witnessed by thousands of people, for which he gave credit to his Father in heaven. Over five hundred people saw him alive after he died and was buried, sealed into a cave tomb by a stone which probably weighed over a ton. The stone was sealed with the Roman seal, and the penalty for breaking it was death. The guard unit (most likely consisting of sixteen soldiers) set by Pilate to keep watch, was under penalty of decimation (every tenth man killed) if they failed in their duty. The notion that someone could come along and steal the body out from under their noses is ridiculous.

Another weighty evidence is the behavior of Jesus' disciples. When Jesus is crucified, they scatter and cower in hiding for fear of the Romans. Yet fifty days later (after they receive the Holy Spirit while praying in Jerusalem), they go out boldly and begin preaching the Good News of Jesus' atoning death and resurrection. No amount of persecution, danger, or hardship deters them. Still today, two thousand years later, millions of Christians around the world remain faithful under the harshest persecution rather than deny their faith in Christ. The details of Jesus' life and death fulfill over one hundred Old Testament (Jewish Bible) prophecies concerning the Messiah, only a few of which Jesus could possibly have orchestrated to happen.

Jesus truly is Lord of heaven and earth, and no one gets to heaven except through faith in him. Do not think that in your own strength and willpower you can clean yourself up from sin. God looks at the heart, and only God can cleanse your heart. Jesus says to you, "The Holy Spirit is now knocking on your heart's door seeking entrance." The Spirit will utterly assure you that the words of Jesus are true and trustworthy when he says: "I love you, and I will wash you clean from your sins in the waters of Holy Baptism. I want you to be with me in heaven."

> Jesus said, "I am the one who brings people back to life, and I am life itself. Those who believe in me will live even if they die. Everyone who lives and believes in me will never die." (John 11:25–26)

If you are an unbeliever or a doubter who has been waffling, not sure about Jesus the Christ's message of salvation, please pray for God to strengthen and increase your nascent faith. Read the Bible yourself; you might begin with John, which contains the largest number of Jesus' own words.

> So faith comes from hearing the message, and the message that is heard is what Christ spoke. (Rom. 10:17)

Read what Jesus has to say in the gospels: Matthew, Mark, Luke, and John. Tell Jesus that he is the Lord of your life and ask him to fill you with his Holy Spirit before it's too late.

> The unfaithful will find themselves in the fiery lake of burning sulfur. (Rev. 21:20)

My friend *Samara was immersed in Islam. As a Muslim living in Afghanistan, she elevated the Prophet Muhammad above Jesus. When a Bible found its way into her hands, Samara was confused. Was Jesus really the Son of God? Could the Quran possibly be wrong?

Samara was angry at herself for doubting the Quran, and put the Bible out of her mind for a couple years, but it found its way back to her. God had chosen her to be his child, but she just hadn't realized it yet! After delving into the Bible again, Samara stayed up praying and crying all night long one night, asking God to please tell her who he is. "If you're Jesus, that's okay; I just want to know," she told God. "If you're not, please forgive me for thinking you might be Jesus." Then, having been taught her whole life to despise Christians and Jews, she muttered and cried to herself, "Please don't be Jesus. Please don't be Jesus. Please don't be Jesus ..."

God showed himself to Samara that night. He told her, "I am the God of Abraham, Isaac and Jacob, the Father of Jesus." On another occasion, Jesus himself appeared to her and told her he was God. Samara immersed herself in the Bible and began worshiping Jesus.

God came to Samara again as she was lying in her bed one night and showed her the heavens. "I knew I wasn't dreaming," she said, "because I kept looking at my arms and legs to make sure I was awake. I couldn't believe that I could see the stars in my bedroom. It was so beautiful!" Samara's bedroom ceiling disappeared and she could see into heaven. God showed her there were only a few of her people in heaven, and she knew, after seeing the vision, that she was to go and witness to her people.

Samara is living in the states now, and witnessing is very difficult for her, because when a Muslim leaves Islam for any other religion, they are considered an infidel by other Muslims who are supposed to kill the traitor. Despite this, Samara has a group of about a dozen Muslim women whom she has been meeting with to share the good news of Jesus' atoning death for our sins.

Samara said her family and close friends are amazed at the blessings God has been pouring down on her since she accepted Jesus as Lord and has turned her life over to him. Of course, as a Christian, she has trials and persecutions as well.

> Jesus said, "It's impossible for people to save themselves, but it's not impossible for God to save them. Everything is possible for God." Then Peter spoke up, "We've given up everything to follow you." Jesus said, "I can guarantee

this truth: Anyone who gave up his home, brothers, sisters, mother, father, children, or fields because of me and the Good News will certainly receive a hundred times as much here in this life. They will certainly receive homes, brothers, sisters, mothers, children and fields, along with persecutions. But in the world to come they will receive eternal life. But many who are first will be last, and the last will be first." (Mark 10:27–30)

If the Holy Spirit is leading you to receive Jesus as your Lord and Savior, you can pray in your own words or use this prayer:

Dear Father, I believe that you sent your Son Jesus to die on the cross for me and that for the sake of his innocent blood you have forgiven all my sins, including my sin of unbelief. I believe you raised Jesus from the dead and that he lives and reigns with you. I promise now to make Jesus Lord of my life, and I believe he has sent his Holy Spirit to live in me so that my life is exchanged for yours lived in me. Fill me with your Holy Spirit, Lord. Increase my faith in you and help me to obey your will as I begin my life as your disciple. I look forward to the day when you will return to take me and all believers to heaven to live with you forever in your glorious kingdom. In Jesus' name I pray. Amen.

19

The Unforgiving

If you forgive the failures of others, your heavenly Father will also forgive you. But if you don't forgive others, your Father will not forgive your failures. (Matt. 6:14–15)

*Barbara has held a grudge against her sister *Diane for over thirty years, and Diane, too, has refused to forgive Barbara for a comment Barbara made long ago about Diane's son. Barbara had judged Diane's son harshly because he had impregnated a woman out of wedlock.

> Stop judging so that you will not be judged. Otherwise, you will be judged by the same standard you use to judge others. The standards you use for others will be applied to you. So why do you see the piece of sawdust in another believer's eye and not notice the wooden beam in your own eye? How can you say to another believer, 'Let me take the piece of sawdust out of your eye,' when you have a beam in your own eye? You hypocrite! First remove the beam from your own eye. Then you will see clearly to remove the piece of sawdust from another believer's eye. (Matt. 7:1–5)

Diane was upset by Barbara's judgment on her son and refused to speak to her sister or have any contact with her again. Barbara, in all her piety, insisted she was right and made no effort to apologize or reach out to her sister until recently. Both women are now in their eighties and were brought together when they attended the funeral of their brother, with whom both had remained close. After the funeral, Barbara wrote a letter to Diane to try to make amends. Diane rejected her sister's apology. In the "Lord's prayer," Jesus instructed us to pray this way:

> Forgive us our sins *because* we have forgiven others. (Matt. 6:12 RPD)

It could not be more clear that if we refuse to forgive, God will not forgive us. Diane, if she does not turn from unforgiveness, is in danger of spending eternity in hell.

Forgiving and forgetting

Since God forgives you all your sins for Jesus' sake, what right do you have *not* to forgive others? God has forgiven me for so many horrible sins I have committed in my life, many of which are included in this book. There are those who have committed some horrible sins against me. How can I not forgive them when Jesus has forgiven me for everything I have done? If I don't forgive them, then God won't forgive me.

Forgiving is one of the hardest things we must do as Christians, and the devil throws many obstacles in our paths to keep us from forgiving people. First, pride always gets in the way. Second, the devil tries to make us think that if we forgive a person, we are saying that what they did was okay. If those don't work, he will try to get us to believe that if we forgive a person, we are enabling bad behavior on their part. The truth is that forgiveness sets *us* free. Harboring unforgiveness or carrying a grudge leads to bitterness and a truly miserable life as well as to heart disease and cancer.[1] Scientific studies have proven that people who are quick to forgive are healthier and live longer than those who are not. Again, God knows what is best for us!

People will say, "There are some things which just can't be forgiven." Those who have had a child murdered say, "You can't possibly understand how I feel. I will never forgive the monster who did this. Never. My child wouldn't want me to."

Jesus understands how you feel, and, yes, your child would want you to forgive the person responsible for their death because your child wants you to spend eternity in heaven. Where would we be if Jesus said to us, "There are some things that just can't be forgiven? Sorry about that, but I just can't forgive you for *that* sin." Jesus forgives all our sins (except for blaspheming the Holy Spirit) and expects us to do the same.

> Put up with each other, and forgive each other if anyone has a complaint. Forgive as the Lord forgave you. (Col. 3:13)

Jesus said we must forgive someone as many times as it takes. We should never stop forgiving someone who has sinned against us. If someone says something to hurt your feelings, you must forgive him. When the same person offends you the following week, you must forgive him again. No matter how difficult it is for the other person to change their behavior, you must continue to forgive him.

What if he doesn't say he's sorry, you ask. Remember, it is the state of *your* heart which is important. You simply need to allow God to work love in your heart for the person. You will be amazed how, as you grow in the Lord, you get to the place where you scarcely even notice most offenses.

> Then Peter came to Jesus and asked him, "Lord, how often do I have to forgive a believer who wrongs me? Seven times?" Jesus answered him, "I tell you, not just seven times, but seventy times seven." (Matt. 18:21–22)

What if I don't *feel* like forgiving him, you ask. Feelings don't matter; forgiveness begins with a decision of your will. You decide to forgive the person because God asks it of you. As you allow the Holy Spirit to work in you through the Great Exchange, your feelings will change over time. Only as you allow his work in you can you come to the place where you "forget" the offense. Can a person forget that their child was murdered? Of course not. That person can, with God's help, reach the place where they no longer feel anger or hatred. Believe it or not, the Holy Spirit's power is great enough even to work love in the parent's heart towards the murderer of their child.

If you claim to have forgiven someone but continually repeat to others what they've done wrong or continually go over in your head what they did, then you have not forgiven them. When a couple was making their wedding plans, a relative threatened that if they invited two couples from a group the husband was involved with at church, then she wouldn't attend the wedding. She was still angry at them for something which had occurred thirty-five years prior. She was aware that the husband had been a member of this group for over twenty years, and he wanted all in the group to attend. He said he couldn't invite some of them to the wedding and not invite all of them. The couple pleaded with this relative, reminding her that she needed to forgive these people for the perceived slight against her from years before. "I have forgiven them," she snapped, "but that doesn't mean I want to be around them."

Forgiveness includes acting in love towards the person, regardless of how we feel. When God forgives us, he actually forgets what we did and does not remember it. God says, "What sin?" To remember means to call it to mind. God never brings it up in his mind again. If we forgive by the power of the Holy Spirit, when the devil tries to bring the offense back to our mind, we are able to say,

"No! I forgive that person. I am not going to think about the bad thing. In fact, I think I will try to remember some good things about that person."

If the objector had truly forgiven these couples, then she would be able to associate with them as if the incident had never happened. Truly God–like forgiveness is that which continues the relationship as if the wrong never happened to disrupt it by the sin or offense. Instead she chose to hold a grudge. When family members or friends disagree, they must be sure to stick to the issue at hand and not bring up past disagreements. True forgiveness means letting go of past wrongs.

Revenge

Some people not only cannot forgive those who have sinned against them, but they want revenge for the wrong they have suffered. They want to pay the sinner back, give him what they think he deserves. Jails are filled with people who have sought revenge, and hell is, too.

> Don't pay people back with evil for the evil they do to you, or ridicule those who ridicule you. Instead, bless them, because you were called to inherit a blessing. (1 Pet. 3:9)

Who really wins when you pay someone back for having wronged you? Since you have earned a ticket to hell for not forgiving the person, the devil wins. Jesus won salvation for you by dying on the cross to forgive all your sins, but to receive that salvation, you must forgive others. Forgiveness isn't optional! The Holy Spirit at work in you can enable you to be willing to forgive.

> Never get revenge. Never hold a grudge against any of your people. Instead, love your neighbor as you love yourself. I am the Lord. (Lev. 19:18)

Jesus tells the parable of the unmerciful servant who owed a king a large sum of money. The king ordered that the man, his wife, children, and all the man owned should be sold to pay the debt. The servant fell on his knees before the king and begged the king to have mercy on him. The king canceled the debt and let the man go.

When the man left, he ran into a fellow servant who owed him a small amount of money. He began choking the man, demanding that he be paid back the debt. The fellow servant begged for mercy, but the man refused and had him thrown in prison until the debt could be paid.

The other servants who had seen what had happened went and told the king. He called the man in and said, "You wicked servant. I canceled all that debt of yours because you begged me to. Shouldn't you have had mercy on your fellow servant just as I had on you?" He turned the servant over to the jailers to be tortured until the debt was paid back.

> Jesus said: That is what my Father in heaven will do to you if each of you does not sincerely forgive other believers. (Matt: 18:35)
>
> You have heard that it was said, 'Love your neighbor, and hate your enemy.' But I tell you this: Love your enemies, and pray for those who persecute you. (Matt: 5:44)
>
> Be kind to each other, sympathetic, forgiving each other as God has forgiven you through Christ. (Eph. 4:32)

Forgiveness before blessings

The very first words Jesus spoke from the cross were, "Father, forgive them. They don't know what they're doing." (Luke 23:34) Jesus' first words, while in unimaginable physical, emotional, and spiritual pain, were neither for himself nor against those who had nailed him to the cross. They were on behalf of his enemies.

If we want God to hear and answer our prayers, we must be willing to forgive—to let go of wrongs done to us. If we want to be set free, we must be willing to set others free. You won't realize all the blessings God has in store for you while you're harboring unforgiveness. If you're having trouble forgiving someone, ask God to soften your heart, to remove the bitterness, and to help you to forgive and love that person. Start praying for the people you need to forgive, asking God to bless them, whether you feel like it or not. Then be prepared to be amazed at the change God makes in your heart and at how much better you feel.

> Jesus says, Whenever you pray, forgive anything you have against anyone. Then your Father in heaven will forgive your failures. (Mark 11:25)

God never asks us to do anything that isn't good for us *and* for others. Unforgiveness poisons our lives, and God wants us to be healthy. Unforgiveness holds others in spiritual bondage, and God wants them to be set free. If you are ready to repent of refusing to forgive and would like to receive God's forgiveness, you can say this prayer.

Dear Father, please forgive me for not forgiving others as you have forgiven me. Soften my heart and help me to sincerely forgive those whom I need to forgive, and help me to act in a loving way towards them. Right now I forgive the following people against whom I have been holding a grudge (name them here). I receive Jesus as my Lord and Savior and look forward to the day when he will return and take me and all believers to heaven to live with you forever in your glorious kingdom. In Jesus' name I pray. Amen.

20

The Vile

Certainly, an evil person will not go unpunished, but the descendants of righteous people will escape. (Prov. 11:21)

If you have found yourself (in the present, not your past) in three or four or five or even more of the chapters in this book, you are the vile (morally despicable or abhorrent) person God is talking about when he says, "Detestable people will find themselves in the fiery lake of burning sulfur." (Rev. 21:8) You obviously have not received Jesus as your Lord and Savior, and you are not in obedience to God's commandments and his will for your life.

Some people are just evil or wicked. Few of them would pick up a book of this nature, but if you're one of them and you have made it this far in the book, you probably recognized yourself in nearly every chapter. Do you want to change your vile ways but haven't known how to do it? Perhaps you have not believed it was possible for you to change. This is exactly why Jesus came: to bust up the works of the devil and to change people's hearts. God loved you before you ever thought about loving him. His Holy Spirit *is* able to help you make the Great Exchange, and he doesn't want anyone to be lost.

> Turn away from evil and do good. Seek peace, and pursue it! The Lord's eyes are on righteous people. His ears hear their cry for help. The Lord confronts those who do evil in order to wipe out all memory of them from the earth. Righteous people cry out. The Lord hears and rescues them from all their troubles. (Ps. 34:14–16)

Many people believe they should live as if today were the first day of the rest of their lives. They want to seize the moment and enjoy all the worldly pleasures. There is a far better way of living. We should live each day as if it were the last day of our life, expecting Jesus to return at any moment.

If we look at the daily headlines, it's obvious Satan has control of a lot of people and that our culture has become desensitized to sin and to the importance of God in our history and national life. Child molesters are so common they don't make the news anymore unless they are a theologian or a prominent citizen. Homosexuals are campaigning for the right to marry. People are lobbying to have God's name removed from our national pledge and from our currency.

Textbooks have been radically altered over the last fifty years. Historical facts that show God's hand in American history have been removed. Many of the people who came to the "new land" from other countries in the seventeenth and eighteenth centuries came to bring the good news of Jesus to the people living in the western hemisphere. Most, if not all, of the men who wrote the *Declaration of Independence* were Christians, but you won't find that information in today's history books. Most of the abolitionists (people who wanted slavery to become illegal) were Christians, and pastors were preaching against slavery from the pulpits of their churches. These are just a small sample of the vital information which has been lost in our schools.

Satan is on a rampage, "knowing his time is short" (Rev. 12:12), and his followers, whether they realize they are following him or not, are increasing in numbers every day. These are the vile God is talking about in the Bible.

> You must understand this: In the last days there will be violent periods of time. People will be selfish and love money. They will brag, be arrogant, and use abusive language. They will curse their parents, show no gratitude, have no respect for what is holy, and lack normal affection for their families. They will refuse to make peace with anyone. They will be slanderous, lack self-control, be brutal, and have no love for what is good. They will be traitors. They will be reckless and conceited. They will love pleasure rather than God. They will appear to have a godly life, but they will not let its power change them. Stay away from such people. (2 Tim. 3:1–5)

It is not too late to give up your evil ways and follow Jesus instead of Satan. God can and will change your heart if you ask him to help you recover from your sinful ways. God doesn't want to see anyone go to hell but wants everyone to repent and receive his grace and mercy.

> Seek the Lord while he may be found. Call on him while he is near. Let wicked people abandon their ways. Let evil people abandon their thoughts. Let them return to the Lord, and he will show compassion to them. Let them return to our God, because he will freely forgive them. (Is. 55:6–7)

Rev. Dr. Ken Rogahn, my pastor friend and mentor whom I wrote about in a previous book, said that when people are involved in evil doings, they're constantly looking over their shoulders. "When you're driving on the highway and you're going the speed limit, you can look around at the sights and enjoy the scenery," Pastor Rogahn said, "but when you're not obeying the speed limit, you're constantly looking in your rearview mirror to see if a police officer is going to catch you. What evildoers forget is that we can look in our 'rearview mirrors'—the consciences God gave us—at any time, and know *God* is watching us. We need to obey all the 'speed limits' of life and live our lives knowing that every evil thing we do is being recorded and that we will one day be judged for our acts."

Jesus died for sinners. He died for the evil, the wicked, the vile. Those are the ones who need a Savior to rescue them from a torturous eternity in hell. Don't ever think your sins are so bad or they are so many that you don't have a chance of going to heaven. Some people go on living an evil life because they think they have done so many bad things that they're already doomed to hell. They don't think anything can change that, so what does it matter what they do? It does matter to God, so that assertion isn't true.

Jesus is ready and waiting for you to repent (truly desire in your heart to change your mind and actions), ask for his forgiveness, and declare that he is now Lord of your life. That's all you have to do—call on his name and ask, and he will save you. If you are ready to do that, you can say this prayer.

Dear Father, please forgive me for living a life that is not pleasing to you. In particular, forgive me for my sins of (name whatever sins the Holy Spirit brings to your mind). I am truly sorry for everything I've done, and I never want to do these things again. I ask you to change my heart so that I can come into obedience to your commandments and your will for my life. Help me to put my full trust in you and to live a life that pleases you. I receive Jesus as my Lord and Savior and look forward to the day when he will return to take me and all believers to heaven to live with you forever in your glorious kingdom. In Jesus' name I pray. Amen.

21

Visions of Hell

Jesus said, "So if your right eye causes you to sin, tear it out and throw it away. It is better for you to lose a part of your body than to have all of it thrown into hell. And if your right hand leads you to sin, cut it off and throw it away. It is better for you to lose a part of your body than to have all of it go into hell." (Matt 5:29–30)

Jesus said, "Don't be afraid of those who kill the body but cannot kill the soul. Instead, fear the one who can destroy both body and soul in hell." (Matt. 10:28)

Jesus said, "Just as weeds are gathered and burned, so it will be at the end of time. The Son of man will send his angels. They will gather everything in his kingdom that causes people to sin and everyone who does evil. The angels will throw them into a blazing furnace. People will cry and be in extreme pain there. Then the people who have God's approval will shine like the sun in their Father's kingdom. Let the person who has ears listen!" (Matt. 13:40–43)

Jesus said, "Then the king will say to those on his left, 'Get away from me! God has cursed you! Go into everlasting fire that was prepared for the devil and his angels! I was hungry, and you gave me nothing to eat. I was thirsty, and you gave me nothing to drink. I was a stranger, and you didn't take me into your homes. I needed clothes, and you didn't give me anything to wear. I was sick and in prison, and you didn't take care of me.'

"They, too, will ask, 'Lord when did we see you hungry or thirsty or as a stranger or in need of clothes or sick or in prison and didn't help you?'

"He will answer them, 'I can guarantee this truth: Whatever you failed to do for one of my brothers or sisters, no matter how unimportant they seemed, you failed to do for me.'

"These people will go away into eternal punishment, but those with God's approval will go into eternal life." (Matt. 25:41–46)

Jesus said, "So if your hand causes you to lose your faith, cut it off! It is better for you to enter life disabled than to have two hands and go to hell, to the fire that cannot be put out. If your foot causes you to lose your faith, cut it off! It is better for you to enter life lame than to have two feet and be thrown into hell. If your eye causes you to lose your faith, tear it out! It is better for you to enter the kingdom of God with one eye than to have two eyes and be thrown into hell. In hell worms that eat the body never die, and the fire is never put out. Everyone will be salted with fire. (Mark 9:43–49)

Jesus said, "There was a rich man who wore expensive clothes. Every day was like a party to him. There was also a beggar named Lazarus who was regularly brought to the gate of the rich man's house. Lazarus would have eaten any scraps that fell from the rich man's table. Lazarus was covered with sores, and dogs would lick them.

"One day the beggar died, and the angels carried him to be with Abraham. The rich man also died and was buried. He went to hell, where he was constantly tortured. As he looked up, in the distance he saw Abraham and Lazarus. He yelled, 'Father Abraham! Have mercy on me! Send Lazarus to dip the tip of his finger in water to cool off my tongue. I am suffering in this fire.'

"Abraham replied, 'Remember, my child, that you had a life filled with good times, while Lazarus' life was filled with misery. Now he has peace here, while you suffer. Besides, a wide area separates us. People couldn't cross it in either direction even if they wanted to.'

"The rich man responded, 'Then I ask you, Father, to send Lazarus back to my father's home. I have five brothers. He can warn them so that they won't end up in this place of torture.'

"Abraham replied, 'They have Moses' Teachings and the Prophets. Your brothers should listen to them!'

"The rich man replied, 'No, Father Abraham! If someone comes back to them from the dead, they will turn to God and change the way they think and act.'

"Abraham answered him, 'If they won't listen to Moses' Teachings and the Prophets, they won't be persuaded even if someone comes back to life.'" (Luke 16:19–31)

Certainly, it is right for God to give suffering to those who cause you to suffer. It is also right for God to give all of us relief from our suffering. He will do this when the Lord Jesus is revealed, coming from heaven with his mighty angels in a blazing fire. He will take revenge on those who refuse to acknowledge God and on those who refuse to respond to the Good News about our Lord Jesus. They will pay the penalty by being destroyed forever, by being separated from the Lord's presence and from his glorious power. This will happen on that day when he comes to be honored among all his holy people and admired by all who have believed in him. This includes you because you believed the testimony we gave you. (2 Thes. 1:6–10)

God didn't spare angels who sinned. He threw them into hell, where he has secured them with chains of darkness and is holding them for judgment.

God didn't spare the ancient world either. He brought the flood on the world of ungodly people, but he protected Noah and seven other people. Noah was his messenger who told people about the kind of life that has God's approval.

God condemned the cities of Sodom and Gomorrah and destroyed them by burning them to ashes. He made those cities an example to ungodly people of what is going to happen to them. Yet, God rescued Lot, a man who had his approval. Lot was distressed by the lifestyle of people who had no principles and lived in sexual freedom. Although he was a man who had God's approval, he lived among the people of Sodom and Gomorrah. Each day was like torture to him as he saw and heard the immoral things that people did.

Since the Lord did all this, he knows how to rescue godly people when they are tested. He also knows how to hold immoral people for punishment on the day of judgment. This is especially true of those who follow their corrupt nature along the path of impure desires and who despise the Lord's authority. (2 Pet. 2:4–9)

The day of the Lord will come like a thief. On that day heaven will pass away with a roaring sound. Everything that makes up the universe will burn and be destroyed. The earth and everything that people have done on it will be exposed.

All these things will be destroyed in this way. So think of the kind of holy and godly lives you must live as you look forward to the day of God and eagerly wait for it to come. When that day comes, heaven will be on fire and will be destroyed. Everything that makes up the universe will burn and melt. But we look forward to what God has promised—a new heaven and a new earth—a place where everything that has God's approval lives. (2 Pet. 3:10–13)

Another angel, a third one, followed them, and said in a loud voice, "Whoever worships the beast or its statue, whoever is branded on his forehead or his hand, will drink the wine of God's fury, which has been poured unmixed into the cup of God's anger. Then he will be tortured by fiery sulfur in the presence of the holy angels and the Lamb. The smoke from their torture will go up forever and ever. There will be no rest day or night for those who worship the beast or its statue, or for anyone branded with its name. (Rev. 14:9–11)

The devil, who deceived them, was thrown into the fiery lake of sulfur, where the beast and the false prophet were also thrown. They will be tortured day and night forever and ever. (Rev. 20:10)

Death and hell were thrown into the fiery lake. (The fiery lake is the second death.) Those whose names were not found in the Book of Life were thrown into the fiery lake. (Rev. 20:14)

But cowardly, unfaithful, and detestable people, murderers, sexual sinners, sorcerers, idolaters, and all liars will find themselves in the fiery lake of burning sulfur. This is the second death. (Rev. 21:8)

22

Visions of Heaven

This is what the Lord God says: I will create a new heaven and a new earth. Past things will not be remembered. They will not come to mind. Be glad, and rejoice forever in what I'm going to create, because I'm going to create Jerusalem to be a delight and its people to be a joy. I will rejoice about Jerusalem and be glad about my people. Screaming and crying will no longer be heard in the city. There will no longer be an infant who lives for only a few days or an old man who doesn't live a long life. Whoever lives to be a hundred years old will be thought of as young. Whoever dies before he is a hundred years old will be cursed as a sinner. They will build houses and live there. They will plant vineyards and eat fruit from them. They will not build homes and have others live there. They will not plant and have others eat from it. My people will live as long as trees, and my chosen ones will enjoy what they've done. They will never again work for nothing. They will never again give birth to children who die young, because they will be offspring blessed by the Lord. The Lord will bless their descendants as well. Before they call, I will answer. While they're still speaking, I will hear. Wolves and lambs will feed together, lions will eat straw like oxen, and dust will be food for snakes. They will not hurt or destroy anyone anywhere on my holy mountain, says the Lord. (Is. 65:17–25)

Jesus said, "Not everyone who says to me, 'Lord, Lord!' will enter the kingdom of heaven, but only the person who does what my Father in heaven wants. Many will say to me on that day, 'Lord, Lord, didn't we prophesy in your name? Didn't we force out demons and do many miracles by the power and authority of your name?' Then I will tell them publicly, 'I've never known you. Get away from me, you evil people.'" (Matt. 7:21–23)

Jesus said, "The kingdom of heaven is like a treasure buried in a field. When a man discovered it, he buried it again. He was so delighted with it that he went away, sold everything he had, and bought that field.

"Also, the kingdom of heaven is like a merchant who was searching for fine pearls. When he found a valuable pearl, he went away, sold everything he had, and bought it." (Matt. 13:44–46)

Jesus said, I will give you the keys of the kingdom of heaven. Whatever you imprison, God will imprison. And whatever you set free, God will set free." (Matt: 16:19)

Jesus answered Nicodemus, "I can guarantee this truth: No one can enter the kingdom of God without being born of water and the Spirit. Flesh and blood give birth to flesh and blood, but the Spirit gives birth to things that are spiritual. Don't be surprised when I tell you that all of you must be born from above. The wind blows wherever it pleases. You hear its sound, but you don't know where the wind comes from or where it's going. That's the way it is with everyone born of the Spirit." (John 3:5–7)

Jesus said, "Don't be troubled. Believe in God, and believe in me. My Father's house has many rooms. If that were not true, would I have told you that I'm going to prepare a place for you? If I go to prepare a place for you, I will come again. Then I will bring you into my presence so that you will be where I am. You know the way to the place where I am going." (John 14:2–4)

We know that if the life we live here on earth is ever taken down like a tent, we still have a building from God. It is an eternal house in heaven that isn't made by human hands. (2 Cor. 5:1)

I know a follower of Christ who was snatched away to the third heaven fourteen years ago. I don't know whether this happened to him physically or spiritually. Only God knows. I know that this person was snatched away to paradise where he heard things that can't be expressed in words, things that humans cannot put into words. (2 Cor. 12:2)

We, however, are citizens of heaven. We look forward to the Lord Jesus Christ coming from heaven as our Savior. Through his power to bring everything under his authority, he will change our humble bodies and make them like his glorified body. (Phil. 3:20–21)

I saw a new heaven and a new earth, because the first heaven and earth had disappeared, and the sea was gone. Then I saw the holy city, New Jerusalem, coming down from God out of heaven, dressed like a bride ready for her husband. I heard a loud voice from the throne say, "God lives with humans! God will make his home with them, and they will be his people. God himself will be with them and be their God. He will wipe every tear from their eyes. There won't be any more death. There won't be any grief, crying, or pain, because the first things have disappeared."

The one sitting on the throne said, "I am making everything new," He said, "Write this: 'These words are faithful and true.'" He said to me, "It has happened! I am the A and the Z, the beginning and the end. I will give a drink from the fountain filled with the water of life to anyone who is thirsty. It won't cost anything. Everyone who wins the victory will inherit these things. I will be their God, and they will be my children. But cowardly, unfaithful, and detestable people, murders, sexual sinners, sorcerers, idolaters, and all liars will find themselves in the fiery lake of burning sulfur. This is the second death."

One of the seven angels who had the seven bowls full of the last seven plagues came to me and said, "Come! I will show you the bride, the wife of the Lamb." He carried me by his power away to a large, high mountain. He showed me the holy city, Jerusalem, coming down from God out of heaven. It had the glory of God. Its light was like a valuable gem, like gray quartz, as clear as crystal. It had a large, high wall with 12 gates. Twelve angels were at the gates. The names of the 12 tribes of Israel were written on the gates. There were three gates on the east, three gates on the north, three gates on the south, and three gates on the west. The wall of the city had 12 foundations. The 12 names of the 12 apostles of the Lamb were written on them.

The angel who was talking to me had a gold measuring stick to measure the city, its gates, and its wall. The city was square. It was as wide as it was long. He measured the city with the stick. It was 12,000 stadia long. Its length, width, and height were the same. He measured its wall. According to human measurement, which the angel was using, it was 144 cubits. Its wall was made of gray quartz. The city was made of pure gold, as clear as glass. The foundations of the city wall were beautifully decorated with all kinds of gems: The first foundation was gray quartz, the second sapphire, the third agate, the fourth emerald, the fifth onyx, the sixth red quartz, the seventh yellow quartz, the eighth beryl, the ninth topaz, the tenth green quartz, the eleventh jacinth, and the twelfth amethyst. The 12 gates were 12 pearls. Each gate was made of one pearl. The street of the city was made of pure gold, as clear as glass.

I did not see any temple in it, because the Lord God Almighty and the Lamb are its temple. The city doesn't need any sun or moon to give it light because the glory of God gave it light. The Lamb was its lamp. The nations will walk in its light, and the kings of the earth will bring their glory into it. Its gates will be open all day. They will never close because there won't be any night there. They will bring the glory and the wealth of the nations into the holy city. Nothing unclean, no one who does anything detestable, and no liars will ever enter it. Only those whose names are written in the Lamb's Book of Life will enter it. (Rev. 21:1–22:5)

Questions for Discussion

Chapter One: The Adulterers

1. Why do you suppose God considers adultery to be so detestable he would punish the sin with eternal damnation?
2. Who is hurt by adultery?
3. Without naming them in a public discussion, do you know anyone who has committed the sin of adultery?
4. How did their unfaithfulness to their spouse affect their marriage?
5. What would you do if you found out your spouse was unfaithful to you and to the vows made to God?
6. Why do you think people commit adultery? Is it about sex or something else?
7. What changed in the past fifty years that has led to a more accepting attitude towards the adulterer?
8. How does the media influence society's view of the adulterer?
9. How do we minister to the adulterer? To those who have been hurt by adultery?
10. Why do you think God considers premarital sex so detestable he would punish the sin with eternal damnation?
11. Do you believe God will really send fornicators to hell on judgment day?
12. If you are currently having premarital relations but would like to be obedient to God, repent, and be forgiven, are you concerned about how it will affect your relationship?
13. How do you think having had premarital sex will affect your relationship with your partner if you marry this person? If you marry someone else?
14. Who is hurt by premarital sex?
15. How does society view a male who is a virgin when he marries? A female?
16. What has changed in the past fifty years that has led to a more accepting attitude towards those who engage in premarital sex?
17. How does the media influence society's view of the fornicator?

Chapter Two: The Cowards

1. Why do you suppose God considers cowards to be so detestable he would punish the sin of cowardliness with eternal damnation?
2. Think of a time when you were very afraid of someone or something. How would the situation have been different if you had called on God for protection?
3. What do you worry about? Has worry helped the problem or situation?
4. Why does God ask that we not be afraid or worry about things?
5. Have you ever witnessed something unjust? What did you do about it?
6. What will happen if Christians don't stand up for God in their cities, schools, and governments?
7. Do you think it was easier for people to proclaim the gospel during the first one hundred years after Jesus' death and resurrection, or is it easier today?
8. Why are people reluctant to get involved when they witness things such as child or spousal abuse or see a child being bullied?
9. How does the media influence our fears and worries?
10. What is one thing you would like to stop worrying about and turn over to God?
11. Who is hurt by cowardliness?
12. Do you believe God will really send cowards to hell on judgment day?
13. Does society view male cowards differently than female cowards?
14. Does God view male cowards differently than female cowards?
15. Why are Christians afraid to share their faith in Christ with others?
16. What might you do to stop being cowardly and boldly stand up for others and for the gospel of Jesus Christ?
17. Are you willing to be inconvenienced, lose your job, or even lose your life because of declaring your faith in Jesus Christ?

Chapter Three: The Disobedient Christians

1. What constitutes a disobedient Christian?
2. Why do disobedient Christians anger God more than non–Christians do?
3. How does being obedient increase our faith in God?
4. In what ways are you in disobedience to God?
5. Was Jesus ever disobedient to his Father?
6. How does being obedient to God bring us peace?
7. Does being obedient to God cause us to lose our unique identities?
8. Do you think your life will be boring if you come into complete obedience to God's will for you?

9. Do you think it was easier for people to be obedient to God during Jesus' time on earth?
10. Who is hurt by disobedience to God?
11. Why do you suppose God detests disobedience so much he requires eternal damnation as the punishment?
12. Do you believe God will really send disobedient Christians to hell on judgment day?
13. Think of a time when you were disobedient to God. How would the situation have been different had you been obedient?
14. Why do you think some Christians choose to be disobedient to God? Are they really Christians?
15. How do we minister to disobedient Christians?

Chapter Four: The Drunkards

1. Have you ever abused alcohol or drugs?
2. Why do people abuse alcohol or drugs?
3. Is alcoholism a disease or an illness?
4. Is there a difference between being a drinker and being a drunkard?
5. Who does the alcoholic or drug addict hurt?
6. Why does it anger God so much when we abuse our bodies with alcohol or drugs?
7. Why do you think God finds drunkards so detestable he requires eternal damnation as the punishment?
8. How does the media influence our views of drugs and alcohol?
9. Do you believe God will really send drunkards to hell on judgment day?
10. Do you think there are more alcoholics and drug addicts today than there were during Jesus' time on earth?
11. Have you ever gotten into trouble while you were using alcohol or drugs? How would the situation have been different had you been sober or straight?
12. Are those who smoke cigarettes abusing their bodies? What do you think God will say to smokers on judgment day?
13. Children of smokers are more likely to smoke than children of non–smokers. Are children of alcoholics and drug addicts more likely than their peers to try alcohol or drugs?
14. How do we keep our children from abusing alcohol or drugs?
15. How do we minister to the alcoholic or drug addict?
16. Luther said: "That upon which you place your trust and rely on is in reality your god." What is the god of the addict? Is it the Triune God?

Chapter Five: The Envious, Jealous, and Covetous

1. What are the differences between envy, jealousy, and covetousness?
2. Which of the three would you consider to be the worst?
3. Why did God make it a commandment not to covet, rather than citing envy or jealousy in his commandment?
4. Name a time when you have been envious, jealous, or covetous. Did these sins of the heart lead you to commit even worse sins?
5. Why do you think God considers these sins to be so detestable he requires eternal damnation as the punishment?
6. Do you believe God will really send the envious, jealous, and covetous to hell on judgment day?
7. How does the media play a role in causing us to feel envy, jealousy, and covetousness?
8. How do we teach our children to avoid these sins of the heart?
9. Do you see envy, jealousy, and covetousness in your church?
10. How do we best minister to a friend who we know is experiencing these sins of the heart?
11. Do you think these sins are seen more today than they were during the time Jesus was on earth?
12. What can you do the next time you find yourself becoming envious, jealous or covetous of something or someone?
13. How does ambition differ from covetousness?
14. Are there any things that are all right to covet? A number of people covet becoming the next president of the United States. Is this sinful coveting?

Chapter Six: The Greedy

1. At what point does the desire to own something become greed?
2. How do we teach our children not to be greedy?
3. How do we best minister to a greedy friend?
4. Do you think people are greedier now than they were during Jesus' time on earth?
5. Why do you think God detests greediness so much he requires eternal damnation as the punishment?
6. Do you believe God will really send the greedy to hell on judgment day?
7. How does the media cater to the greedy?
8. Name a time when you or someone you know has been greedy. Did that greed lead to worse sins?

9. Why does Jesus say it will be hard for a rich person to get to heaven?
10. How do we store up treasures in heaven?
11. Does everything we own belong to God?
12. Does God bless people with wealth and possessions?
13. Is failure to tithe a form of greed?
14. Why do some people feel a need for greed?
15. How can Jesus replace that need?

Chapter Seven: The Hateful

1. What is righteous anger?
2. Have you or has someone you know ever gone into a fit of rage? Was the anger righteous anger?
3. Is there any discord, dissentions, or factionalism in your home?
4. Is there any discord, dissentions, or factionalism in your church?
5. Do you know anyone who constantly tries to keep things stirred up?
6. Why do you think God considers hatefulness so detestable he requires eternal damnation as the punishment?
7. Do you believe God will really send hateful people to hell on judgment day?
8. Does the media influence people to be more hateful?
9. How do we teach our children to be more loving?
10. How do we minister to someone who is hateful?
11. Are people more hateful today than they were during the days when Jesus was on earth?
12. Do you think it's necessary for people to express their love in words?
13. Is it possible to really love God but to be hateful to other people?
14. Is it okay to hate those from other countries who want to destroy us?
15. Why do some people hate others simply because they're different from them?

Chapter Eight: The Homosexuals

1. Can someone be both a homosexual and a Christian?
2. Do you believe someone is born homosexual?
3. Can Jesus really deliver someone from homosexuality?
4. Why isn't someone who becomes a Christian magically delivered from homosexuality the moment they accept Christ?
5. Are alcoholics, adulterers, and gossipers magically delivered from their bondage when they become Christians?
6. Is it discrimination for states not to allow homosexuals to marry?

7. Why do you think God considers homosexual behavior so detestable he requires eternal damnation as the punishment?
8. Do you believe God will really send homosexuals to hell on judgment day?
9. How does the media influence our views of homosexual behavior?
10. How do we minister to the homosexual?
11. Is homosexual behavior worse than other sins?
12. Who do homosexuals hurt with their sin?
13. What if a person with homosexual tendencies and desires remains celibate? Are they still committing a sin?
14. How does the transvestite sin?
15. Is it a sin to have a sex change operation?

Chapter Nine: The Idolaters

1. Why did God choose to forbid idolatry as the very First Commandment?
2. Are the gods of Islam, Buddhism, and other religions the same god as God the Father of Jesus?
3. Is God turning his back on America because so many are worshiping false gods?
4. Other than false gods, what are some other idols people worship?
5. Who is hurt by idolatry?
6. Why does God consider idolatry so detestable that he requires eternal damnation as the punishment?
7. Do you believe God will really send idolaters to hell on judgment day?
8. How does the media, especially movies and television, influence our views of idolatry?
9. How do we teach our children to avoid idolatry?
10. Are people more idolatrous today than when Jesus was on the earth?
11. How do we minister to the idolater?
12. Can possessions really be considered idolatry? Do idolaters really worship their possessions?
13. Is not placing God first in your life idolatry?
14. Why is the deliberate and willful breaking of any commandment a form of idolatry?

Chapter Ten: The Immoral

1. How would you define "immorality?"
2. What is the difference between *immoral* and *amoral*?
3. Why does God say immoral people are idolaters?

4. Why does God tell us we shouldn't associate with an immoral person who calls himself a Christian?
5. Is God angered more by the immoral Christian than the immoral person who is not a Christian?
6. Who is hurt by immorality?
7. How does the media influence our views of immorality?
8. Why does God consider the immoral so detestable he requires eternal damnation as the punishment?
9. Do you believe God will really send the immoral to hell on judgment day?
10. How do we teach our children to live moral lives?
11. How do we minister to the immoral person?
12. Are people more immoral today than when Jesus walked on the earth?
13. Are people more immoral today than they were fifty years ago?

Chapter Eleven: The Impure

1. How would you define impurity?
2. What is the difference between immorality and impurity?
3. Who is pure enough to enter heaven?
4. Why does Jesus say we must become like a small child to enter heaven?
5. Are all small children pure?
6. Is there such a thing as *original sin?* If so, how would you define it?
7. How do we become pure enough to enter heaven?
8. Why do you think God considers the impure so detestable that he requires eternal damnation as the punishment?
9. Do you believe God will really send the impure to hell on judgment day?
10. How does the media influence our views of the impure?
11. How do we minister or witness to the impure?
12. Are people more impure now than when Jesus walked on the earth?
13. Are people more impure now than they were fifty years ago?
14. Does God want Christians to associate with impure Christians? Why or why not?
15. Knowing what you know, is there such a person as an *impure* Christian?
16. How do we teach our children to live lives that are pure?

Chapter Twelve: The Liars

1. What is the difference between a made-up story and a lie?
2. Is there ever a time when telling a lie is better than telling the truth?

3. How do we make a judgment when no matter what we do will break a commandment?
4. Have you ever been deceived by someone? How did it feel?
5. Have you ever been the subject of someone's gossip? If so, how did it affect you?
6. Has anyone ever given false testimony about you? Would you consider it to be slander?
7. Why does God consider liars to be so detestable that he requires eternal damnation as the punishment?
8. Do you think God will really send liars to hell on judgment day?
9. How does the media influence our views of liars?
10. Liar jokes abound about politicians and lawyers. Are most politicians and lawyers liars? Is it okay to lie in their chosen professions?
11. Are there more liars today than when Jesus walked on the earth?
12. How do we teach our children to be truthful?
13. How do we minister or witness to the liar?
14. Does the liar hurt anyone other than himself or herself?
15. What are some reasons people lie? Do any of the reasons justify their lying?
16. Have you ever been caught in a lie? What did you do?

Chapter Thirteen: The Murderers

1. What are some of the sins that often precede murder?
2. Is thinking about murder as bad as actually murdering someone?
3. What is the difference between a temptation to sin and a sin of thought?
4. Are there more murders today than there were when Jesus walked on the earth?
5. Are there more murders today than there were fifty years ago? Why?
6. How does the media influence our views of murder?
7. Why does God consider abortion to be murder? Assisted suicide? Euthanasia?
8. Can you think of some things which are legal but not morally right?
9. Is murder ever justified? Is killing during wartime the same as murder? What about self-defense?
10. Why does God consider murder to be so detestable that he requires eternal damnation as the punishment?
11. Do you believe God will really send murderers to hell on judgment day? How about those women who have had abortions?
12. Who is hurt by murder?
13. Who is hurt by an abortion?
14. Why do you think our society decided to legalize abortion?

15. What do you think happens to all the babies who have been murdered through abortion?

Chapter Fourteen: Those Who Practice Magic Arts

1. Have you ever consulted a psychic? Was she 100 percent accurate in what she told you?
2. Did the psychic know your name and address before being told?
3. Why do you think consulting horoscopes angers God?
4. Why is God angered as much by white witches as by black witches?
5. When, where, and by whom was Wicca invented?
6. Who do you think mediums are contacting when they claim to contact your dead friends and relatives?
7. Have you ever played with a Ouija Board? Why is a Ouija Board not really considered a game?
8. What superstitions do you follow? Why does this anger God?
9. Why do you think someone would visit a psychic or medium rather than going to God, the only omniscient One?
10. How does the media influence our views of psychics, mediums, and witches?
11. Who is hurt when someone visits a psychic?
12. Why do you think God considers practicing magic arts so detestable that he requires eternal damnation as the punishment?
13. Do you believe God will really send these people to hell on judgment day?
14. Were psychics and witches more prevalent during the time Jesus walked the earth? 15. What about astrologers? Superstitions?
16. How do we teach our children to avoid the magic arts?
17. Should Christian children be reading the Harry Potter books? Why or why not?

Chapter Fifteen: The Selfish

1. Why do the authors say that being rich does not equal being selfish? Do you agree?
2. In what ways can the poor be guilty of selfish ambitions?
3. Do people really reap what they sow? Name an instance when you have blessed someone with something and were blessed by God for your generosity.
4. Is it selfish not to tithe?
5. Name an instance when you have been selfish. How would you handle the situation differently now?

6. Why does God consider selfish ambitions so detestable that he requires eternal damnation as the punishment?
7. Do you believe God will really send the selfish to hell on judgment day?
8. How does the media influence our views of those with selfish ambitions?
9. How do we teach our children not to be selfish?
10. Are people more selfish today than when Jesus walked the earth?
11. Are people more selfish today than fifty years ago?
12. Who is hurt by selfishness?
13. Why are illegal immigrants said to have selfish ambitions?

Chapter Sixteen: The Sexually Immoral

1. Prostitution is legal in parts of Nevada. Do you think it should be legal everywhere?
2. Does a woman have a right to do with her body what she wants?
3. Why is frigidity in marriage considered a sexually immoral sin?
4. The Roman Catholic Church teaches that sexual intercourse is the original sin. Is this correct?
5. Can child molesters be rehabilitated, or should they forever be locked away from children?
6. Why does God find sexual immorality so detestable that he requires eternal damnation as the punishment?
7. Do you believe God will really send the sexually immoral to hell on judgment day?
8. Who is hurt by bestiality? Child molestation? Incest? Prostitution? Frigidity? Pornography?
9. Does sexual lust really lead to other sexual sins?
10. How does the media influence our views of sexual immorality?
11. How do we teach our children to be sexually moral?
12. Is sexual immorality more prevalent today than when Jesus walked on the earth?
13. Is sexual immorality worse today than fifty years ago?

Chapter Seventeen: The Thieves

1. What is the difference between thieves and swindlers? Do you think one is worse than the other?
2. Is lying a form or type of stealing?
3. Have you ever taken something from work? Why does it not seem like stealing when we take from our employers?

4. Have you ever been swindled by someone?
5. Why is failure to tithe a form of stealing?
6. Who is hurt by the actions of thieves and swindlers?
7. Who is hurt when we refuse to tithe?
8. Why do you think God considers thieves and swindlers so detestable that he requires eternal damnation as the punishment?
9. Do you believe God will really send thieves and swindlers to hell on judgment day? What about those who don't tithe?
10. Do you believe God will really pour blessings down on you if you tithe?
11. How does the media influence our views of thieves and swindlers?
12. Is there a difference between sins of weakness and sins of will?
13. How does disruptive behavior in the classroom steal from all the students who want to learn?
14. How do we teach our children not to steal from others?
15. How do we teach our children to tithe?

Chapter Eighteen: The Unbelievers

1. How do we increase our faith in Jesus as Lord?
2. If faith or trust is quantified, how much faith does it take to enter heaven?
3. Why does God find unbelievers so detestable that he requires eternal damnation as the punishment?
4. Do you believe God will really send unbelievers to hell on judgment day?
5. Who do unbelievers hurt?
6. How does the media influence our views of unbelievers?
7. Is believing in Jesus all that is required for admittance to heaven?
8. The Bible says that the devils believe in God. Why aren't they saved too?
9. What is the difference between *saying* we believe and actual faith?
10. How do we teach faith to our children?
11. Why is it so hard for us, like Thomas, to believe in something we haven't seen?
12. How do we reach our unbelieving friends and neighbors with the good news of Jesus' salvation for all?

Chapter Nineteen: The Unforgiving

1. In the Old Testament how did God illustrate forgiveness on the Day of Atonement?
2. Is there someone in your life whom you need to forgive?
3. How does sinful pride get in the way of forgiveness?

4. Why do people feel a need to seek revenge against someone who has wronged them?
5. What do we gain by holding a grudge?
6. Who is hurt when we refuse to forgive someone?
7. How does the media influence our views of those who don't forgive?
8. Why does God consider those who refuse to forgive others so detestable that he requires eternal damnation as the punishment?
9. Do you believe God will really send the unforgiving to hell on judgment day?
10. How do we teach our children to be forgiving?
11. Is there someone who needs to forgive you but hasn't? Have you asked for their forgiveness?
12. Are some sins so bad that God won't forgive them?
13. Has someone done something to you that is so bad you can't forgive them?
14. Who benefits the most when forgiveness is given?

Chapter Twenty: The Vile

1. How would you define "vile" in today's world?
2. How does being vile differ from mere rudeness?
3. Are people more vile today than they were when Jesus walked on the earth?
4. Are people more vile today than fifty years ago?
5. Why does God find the vile so detestable that he requires eternal damnation as the punishment?
6. Who is hurt by the vile?
7. How does the media influence our views of the vile?
8. How do we keep our children from becoming vile?
9. Is every sin mentioned in this book a vile sin?
10. Have you ever done something that would be considered vile?

Suggested Readings

Adultery

Hedges: Loving Your Marriage Enough to Protect It, by Jerry B. Jenkins, Crossway Books, June 2005.
Unfaithful: Rebuilding Trust After Infidelity, by Gary & Mona Shriver, Life Journey, May 2005.
Adultery: The Forgivable Sin, by Bonnie Eaker Weil, Hudson House Publishing, Aug. 2003.
Before You Live Together by David Gudgel, Regal Books, Aug. 2003.
Why Some Christians Commit Adultery: Causes and Curses, by John L. Sanford, Victory House Publishers, Nov. 1989.

Cowards

Love Is Letting Go of Fear, by Gerald G. Jampolsky, Ten Speed Press, April 2004.
The Culture of Fear: Why Americans Are Afraid of the Wrong Things, by Barry Glassner, Basic Books, May 2000.
Share Jesus Without Fear, by William Fay, Broadman & Holman, June 1999.
Witnessing Without Fear, by Bill Bright, Nelson Books, Sept. 1992.
Afraid God Works Afraid He Doesn't, by Terry Rush, Howard Publishing, June 1991.

Disobedient Christians

The Perfect Christian: How Sinners Like Us Can Be More Like Jesus, by Tony Evans, W Publishing Group, Oct. 2000.
When a Christian Sins, by John R. Rice, Sword of the Lord, Aug. 2000.
Grace Abounding ... to the Chief of Sinners, by John Bunyan, Evangelical Press, July 2000.
Maintaining The Delicate Balance In Christian Living: Biblical Balance In A World That's Tilted Toward Sin, by Jay E. Adams, Timeless Texts, Dec. 1998.
Why Christians Sin: Avoiding the Dangers of an Uncommitted Life, by J. Kirk Johnston, Discovery House Publishers, April 1992.

Drunkards

Alcohol, Addiction and Christian Ethics, by Christopher C.H. Cook, Cambridge University Press, June 2006.
When Someone You Love Abuses Drugs Or Alcohol: Daily Encouragement, by Cecil Murphey, Beacon Hill Press, Aug. 2004.
This is Alcohol, by Nick Brownlee, Sanctuary Publishing, Oct. 2002.
There Is a Ram in the Bush: Understanding the Process of Christian Alcohol & Drug Recovery, by Ronald Simmons, Milligan Books, Aug. 1998.
Of Course You're Angry: A Guide to Dealing With the Emotions of Substance Abuse, by Gayle Rosellin & Mark Worden, Hazelden, March 1997.

Envious

Overcoming Envy, by Dr. Windy Dryden, Sheldon Press, June 2003.
Envy: The Enemy Within, by Bob Sorge, Regal Books, Feb. 2003.
Overcoming Jealousy, by Dr. Windy Dryden, Sheldon Press, Jan. 1999.
The Psychology of Jealousy and Envy, by Peter Salovey, The Guilford Press, Feb. 1991.
Overcoming Jealousy and Possessiveness, by Paul A. Hauck, Westminister John Knox Press, Sept. 1981.

Greedy

The True Stella Awards, by Randy Cassingham, Dutton Adult, Nov. 2005.
Anatomy of Greed: The Unshredded Truth from an Enron Insider, by Brian Couver, Carrolls Graf Publishers, Sept. 2002.
Greed: Economics and Ethics in Conflict, by James M. Childs Jr., Augsburg Fortress Publishers, Feb. 2000.
How to Get Really Rich: A Sharp Look at the Religion of Greed, by Brian Rosner, Inter–Varsity Press, Oct. 1999.
The Complete Book of Greed: The Strange and Amazing Story of Human Excess, by M. Hirsh Goldberg, William Morrow & Co., 1994.

Hateful

A Quagmire of Hate: The Post–Election Liberals, by Robin Mullins Boyd, PublishAmerica, Oct. 2005.
Hate–work: Working Through the Pain and Pleasures of Hate, by David W. Augsburger, Westminster John Knox Press, Feb. 2004.

Hatred: The Psychological Descent into Violence, by Willard Gaylin, Public Affairs, Apr. 2003.
Why We Hate, by Rush Dozier, Jr., McGraw–Hill, June 2003.
Prisoners of Hate: The Cognitive Basis of Anger, Hostility, and Violence, by Aaron T. Beck, Harper Paperbacks, Apr. 2003.

Homosexuals

Lord, Take Me and Make Something Beautiful: A One–Year Journey of Deliverance from Homosexuality, by Star Burch, PublishAmerica, Aug. 2005.
Loving Homosexuals As Jesus Would: A Fresh Christian Approach, by Chad W. Thompson, Brazos Press, Dec. 2004.
Closing the Closet: Testimonies of Deliverance from Homosexuality, by Talbert W. Swan, II. Trumpet in Zion Pub., July 2004.
Portraits of Freedom: 14 People Who Came Out of Homosexuality, by Bob Davies and Lela Gilbert, InterVarsity Press, June 2001.
Coming Out of Homosexuality: New Freedom for Men & Women, by David Gudgel, InterVarsity Press, Jan. 1994.

Idolators

Be Saved From the Curses of Idolatry, by Asaph C. Phillips, Xulon Press, Sept. 2005.
Snakes In The Temple: Unmasking Idolatry In Today's Church And Pointing The Way To Spiritual Breakthrough, by David Orton, Send the Light, Inc., Sept. 2004.
Equipped to Love: Idolatry–free Relationships, by Norm Wakefield, Spirit of Elijah Ministries, 2001.
Hard–Core Idolatry: Facing the Facts, by C. Peter Wagner, Wagner Publications Inc., Jan. 1999.
Gods That Fail: Modern Idolatry & Christian Mission, by Vinoth Ramachandra, InterVarsity Press, July 1997.

Immoral

Moral Man and Immoral Society: A Study of Ethics and Politics, by Reinhold Niebuhr, Westminster John Knox Press, Jan. 2002.
Learning to Resist Temptation: In an Immoral Society, by Colin N. Peckham, Christian Focus Publications, July 1999.

Bringing Up Moral Children: In an Immoral World, by A. Lyn Scoresby, Deseret Book Company, Apr. 1998.
Why Good People Do Bad Things: How to Make Moral Choices in an Immoral World, by Bruce Hamstra, Carol Publishing House, July 1996.
Legislating Immorality: The Homosexual Movement Comes Out of the Closet, by George Grand and Mark A. Horne, Moody Pr., Sept. 1993.

Impure

Raising Pure Kids in an Impure World, by Richard & Renee Durfield, Bethany House Publishers, May 2004.
Becoming a Woman of Discretion: Cultivating a Pure Heart in a Sensual World, by Nancy Leigh DeMoss, Life Action Ministries, Apr. 2003.
Raising Sexually Pure Kids: How to Prepare Your Children for The Act of Marriage, by Tim Lahaye, Multnomah, Sept. 1998.
Changes That Heal, by Dr. Henry Cloud, Zondervan, Dec. 1993.
Intimate Deception: Escaping the Trap of Sexual Impurity, by P. Roger Hillerstrom, Multnomah Pub., March 1989.

Liars

Big Fat Liars: How Politicians, Corporations, and the Media use Science and Statistics To Manipulate the Public, by Morris E. Chafetz, Nelson Current, July 2005.
Gossip: Ten Pathways to Eliminate It From Your Life and Transform Your Soul, by Lori Palatnik with Bob Burg, Simcha Press, Aug. 2002.
Stop the Runaway Conversation: Take Control over Gossip and Criticism, by Michael De. Sedler, Chosen Books, May 2001.
Lying: Moral Choice in Public and Private Life, by Sissela Bok, Vintage, Sept. 1999.
Lying and Deception in Everyday Life, by Michael Lewis and Carolyn Saarni, The Guilford Press, Feb. 1993.

Murderers

The Case Against Assisted Suicide, Edited by Kathleen M. Foley and Herbert Hendin, The Johns Hopkins University Press, May 2004.
How Can We Forgive Murderers?: And Other Answers To Questions About a Course in Miracles, by Greg Mackie, Circle Publishing, Apr. 2003.
Mass Murder in the United States, by Ronald M. Holmes and Stephen T. Holmes, Prentice Hall, Aug. 2000.

Euthanasia and Physician–Assisted Suicide: Killing or Caring? by Michael Manning, Paulist Press, Sept. 1998.
Abortion: The Silent Holocaust, by John Joseph Powell, Tabor Pub., Nov. 1981.

Magic Arts

Protect Your Teen From Today's Witchcraft: A Parent's Guide to Confronting Wicca and the Occult, by Steve Russo, Bethany House Publishers, Sept. 2005.
Dewitched: What You Need to Know About the Dangers of Witchcraft and Wicca, by Tim Baker, W Publishing Group, Sept. 2004.
Witchcraft Goes Mainstream: Uncovering Its Alarming Impact On You and Your Family, by Brooks Alexander, Harvest House Publishers, Sept. 2004.
Overcoming Witchcraft, by Rick Joyner, Morningstar Publications (NC), June 1996.
Destroying the Works of Witchcraft Through Fasting & Prayer, by Ruth Brown, Impact Christian Books, Dec. 1994.

Selfish

Denying One's Self in a Selfish World by James E. Puckett, Infinity Pub., June 2005.
The Epidemic: The Rot of American Culture, Absentee and Permissive Parenting, and the Resultant Plague of Joyless, Selfish Children, by Robert Shaw, Regan Books, Oct. 2004.
Beyond Tithes & Offerings, by Michael L. Webb and Mitchell T. Webb, On Time Publishing, Dec. 1998.
Stacked Deck: A Story of Selfishness in America, by Lawrence E. Mitchell, Temple University Press, Apr. 1998.
Struggling With Selfishness, by Woodrow M. Knoll, Back to the Bible Publishing, Sept. 1996.

Sexually Immoral

Confronting Pornography: A Guide to Prevention and Recovery for Individuals, Loved Ones, and Leaders, by Mark D. Chamberlain, Deseret Book Company, July 2005.
Sex And The Single Guy: Winning Your Battle For Purity, by Joseph Knable, Moody Publishers, March 2005.
How Far Is Too Far? Where to Draw the Line On Premarital Sex and Physical Intimacy, by Todd Lochner, Brown Books, Oct. 2004.

Sex, Demons and Morality, by Peter Hobson, Impact Christian Books, Dec. 1998.
Sex in the Christian Marriage, by Richard Meier, Paul Meier, and Frank Minirth, Fleming H. Revel Company, March 1997.

Thieves

Pyromania, Kleptomania, and Other Impulse–Control Disorders, by Julie Williams, Enslow Publishers, Sept. 2002.
Frauds, Deceptions, and Swindles, by Carl Sifakis, Checkmark Books, Apr. 2001.
Stealing Jesus: How Fundamentalism Betrays Christianity, by Bruce Bawer, Three Rivers Press, Oct. 20, 1998.
Kleptomania: The Compulsion to Steal—What Can Be Done, by Marcus J. Goldman, M.D., New Horizon Press, Oct. 1997.
Bring the Full Tithe: Sermons on the Grace of Giving, by William D. Watley, Judson Press, March 1995.

Unbelievers

I Don't Have Enough Faith to Be an Atheist, by Norm L. Geisler and Frank Turek, Crossway Books, Feb. 2004.
No Wonder They Call Him the Savior: Experiencing the Truth of the Cross, by Max Lucado, W. Publishing Group, Feb. 2004.
The New Evidence That Demands A Verdict Fully Updated To Answer The Questions Challenging Christians Today, by Josh McDowell, Nelson Reference, Oct. 1999.
The Case for Christ: A Journalist's Personal Investigation of the Evidence for Jesus, by Lee Strobel, Zondervan, Sept. 1998.
More Than a Carpenter, by Josh McDowell, Tyndale House Publishers, Apr. 1987.

Unforgiving

The Power of Forgiving, by Everett L. Worthington, Templeton Foundation Press, Oct. 2005.
Forgiving Your Family: A Journey To Healing, by Kathleen Fischer, Upper Room Books, June 2005.
Forgiving and Reconciling: Bridges to Wholeness and Hope, by Everett L. Worthington, InterVarsity Press, Aug. 2003.
Total Forgiveness by R.T. Kendall, Charisma House, Aug. 2002.

From Forgiven to Forgiving: Learning to Forgive One Another God's Way, by Jay Adams, Calvary Press, Nov. 1997.

Vile

Abundant Living for Christians, by Arthur Stevens, Xulon Press, Feb. 2005.
If God Has a Refrigerator, Your Picture Is On It, by James W. Moore, Dimensions for Living, March 2003.
New Believers: Guide to Effective Christian Living, by Greg Laurie, Tyndale House Publishers, July 2002.
After "I Believe:" Experiencing Authentic Christian Living, by Mark D. Roberts, Baker Books, March 2002.
Morality: An Invitation to Christian Living, by Joseph Stoutzenberger, Harcourt Religious Publishers, Oct. 2000.

Visions of Hell

23 Minutes in Hell, by Bill Wiese, Charisma House, March 2006.
God Can Not Be Trusted (and Five Other Lies of Satan), by Terry Evans, Multnomah, Sept. 2005.
To Hell and Back: Life After Death Startling New Evidence by Maurice S. Rawlings, M.D., Thomas Nelson, Feb. 1996.
Hell on Trial: The Case for Eternal Punishment, by Robert A. Peterson, P & R Publishing, July 1995.
A Divine Revelation of Hell, by Mary K. Baxter, Whitaker House, Sept. 1993.

Visions of Heaven

Heaven, by Randy C. Alcorn, Tyndale House Publishers, Oct. 2004.
90 Minutes In Heaven: A True Story of Death & Life, by Don Piper with Cecil Murphey, Revell, Sept. 2004.
Heaven Is So Real, by Choo Thomas, Creation House, Oct. 2003.
A Divine Revelation of Heaven, by Mary K. Baxter, Whitaker House, July 1998.
Visions of Heaven by H.A. Baker, Whitaker House, June 1973.

References

Chapter One: The Adulterers

1. Hrenchir, Tim, "Unholy alliance." *The Topeka Capital–Journal.* CJ–Online, Oct. 21, 2006.
2. Langley, Alison, "Death Penalty: Seven Women Face Stoning in Iran." *Inter Press Service News Agency,* Sept. 29, 2006.
3. Fryling, Alice, "Why Wait for Sex?" Intervarsity Christian Fellowship/USA *Student Leadership Journal,* Spring 1995.
4. Demaris, Alfred and Rao. K.V., "Premarital Cohabitation and the Subsequent Marital Stability in the United States: A Reassessment." *Journal of Marriage and the Family,* 1992.

Chapter Two: The Cowards

1. "Quoteworthy," Focus on the Family, *Citizenlink.com,* Nov. 6, 2006.
2. Stoeckeler, Keith, "Helping others is not an easy feat." *The Marlin Chronicle,* Oct. 1, 2004.
3. Crice, Elizabeth, "Turning a blind eye: New BBC series highlights the disturbing culture of the bystander." *Electronic Telegraph,* Nov. 1, 1997.
4. See Note 3 above.
5. Scheenberger, Gary, "Barking Up The Wrong Tree." Focus on the Family, *Citizenlink.com,* Sept. 19, 2006.
6. Falwell, Jerry, "Graduates: We Will Not Be Silenced." *The Conservative Voice,* May 26, 2006.
7. Toland, Bill, "In–your–face evangelist challenges hate–crime law's limits." *Pittsburgh Post Gazette,* Jan. 23, 2005.
8. King, Suzanne, "Sins of omission." *Ryerson Review of Journalism,* Summer 1999.
9. Knight, Robert. "Christian Business Ordered to Duplicate Homosexual Activist Videos." *Culture and Family Institute,* Apr. 25, 2006.
10. Hirsen, James, "Stephen Baldwin Battles Porn Shop." *NewsMax.com,* Mar. 28, 2006.
11. White, Tom, *The Voice of the Martyrs,* Oct. 18, 2006.

Chapter Three: The Disobedient Christians

1. "Church forces out Haggard for 'sexually immoral' conduct." *CNN.com* Nov. 4, 2006.
2. Chu, Jeff, "10 Questions For Katharine Jefferts Schori." *Time*, July 17, 2006.
3. Bakker, Jim, *I Was Wrong: The Untold Story of the Shocking Journey from PTL Power to Prison and Beyond*, Nelson Books, Oct. 1997.

Chapter Four: The Drunkards

1. Caruso, Michelle, "Mel gives cops hell." *New York Daily News*, July 29, 2006.
2. Breznican, Anthony, "Gibson apologizes for 'despicable' remarks." *USA Today*, July 29, 2006

Chapter Five: The Envious, Jealous, and Coveteous

1. Judge, Dan. "Who gets a lump of coal this year?" *Times–Herald*, Dec. 11, 2005.

Chapter Six: The Greedy

1. McNeill, David, "Still Angry After All These Years." *The Independent*, Feb. 25, 2006.
2. Pacelle, Mitchell, "Despite Lawsuit Enron Bonuses Remain Unreturned." *Wall Street Journal*, Nov. 2, 2003.
3. Held, Tom, "Gesu bookkeeper faces charges of taking $500,000 from church." *Milwaukee Journal Sentinel*, Oct. 18, 2003.
4. "Pittsburgh Priest Charged With Stealing $1.5 Million." *Catholic World News*, Aug. 13, 1998.
5. Cassingham, Randy, *The True Stella Awards: Honoring real cases of greedy opportunists, frivolous lawsuits, and the law run amok*, Dutton Adult, Nov. 2005.

Chapter Seven: The Hateful

1. Cropper, Carol Marie, "Black Man Fatally Dragged In a Possible Racial Killing." *The New York Times*, June 10, 1998.
2. Seenan, Gerard, "4 Years for woman who killed over parking space." *The Guardian*, Nov. 5, 2005.
3. "Suspect in bridge drowning to stand trial." *CNN News Briefs*, Sept. 1, 1995.
4. Stannard, Matthew B., "Road–rage dog tosser sentenced to 3 years. Judge throws book at Leo's killer." *San Francisco Chronicle*, July 14, 2001.

5. "Universal Studios Pulls 'Boys are Stupid' T–Shirts in Face of Radio Campaign." *Men's News Daily*, Jan. 13, 2004.

Chapter Eight: The Homosexuals

1. Whitehead, N.E., Ph.D., "The Importance of Twin Studies." National Association for Research & Therapy of Homosexuality, Apr. 20, 2006.
2. "President Koocher Says the American Psychology Association Has No Disagreement With the Treatment of Unwanted Homosexual Attraction." Aug. 12, 2006.
3. Morrison, Keith, "To hell and back." *Dateline NBC News*, Aug. 13, 2006.
4. Burch, Star, *Lord, Take Me and Make Something Beautiful: A One–Year Journey of Deliverance from Homosexuality*, PublishAmerica, Aug. 2005.

Chapter Nine: The Idolators

1. Sher, Khan, "Allah in a Tomato … and in e–Colie?" *FaithFreeedom.org*, Apr. 8, 2006.
2. Martin, Allie, "Methodist pastor: Christians should respond in 'humility' regarding pope's comments." *OneNewsNow.com*, July 13, 2007.

Chapter Ten: The Immoral

1. Wildmon, Donald E., "The National Education Association: What Kind Of Organization Is This Which Sets The Agenda For Our Children in Public Schools?" *American Family Association*, July 21, 2006.
2. Wildmon, Donald E., "Ford Continues Support For Homosexual Groups." *American Family Association*, July 11, 2006.

Chapter Twelve: The Liars

1. Chavez, Linda, "The yin and yang of media bias stories." *Jewish World Review*, Jan. 12, 2005.

Chapter Thirteen: The Murderers

1. Malvasio, Joe, "Father of Two Robbed and Murdered On Way Home From Work." *NY1 News*, Sept. 4, 2006.
2. Hunt, Stephen, "Hacking appears in court; prelim hearing set." *The Salt Lake Tribune*, Apr. 15, 2005.
3. Baker, Russ, "School Shootings in Perspective: Local Representatives in Denial." *RussBaker.com*, Mar/Apr. 2001.

4. Koidin, Michelle, "Cheerleader mom freed after serving six months." *Abilene Reporter–News*, Mar. 1, 1997.
5. Hollman, Holly, "Wife in love affair admits to murder." *The Decatur Daily*, Mar. 29, 2006.
6. Jarvis, Daniel W., "Is War a Sin?" *AbsoluteTruth.net*
7. "Terri's tube removed: judge ignores Congress." *Catholic World News*, Mar.18, 2005.

Chapter Fourteen: Those Who Practice Magic Arts

1. "School Says Halloween Disrespectful to Witches." *ABC News*, Puyallup, WA, Oct. 21, 2004.
2. "Reiki teachers hit back at priest's Satanic warning." *Breaking News.ie,* Mar. 9, 2006.

Chapter Fifteen: The Selfish

1. "Ethics Violations in Duke Lacrosse Case," *Foxnews.com,* Jun. 17, 2007.

Chapter Sixteen: The Sexually Immoral

1. "Child Molester Statistics." Yellow Dyno Child Protection Specialists.
2. "Online porn addiction turns our kids into victims and predators." The *Sun–Herald*, Aug. 14, 2005.
3. Scott, Shirley Lynn, "Monsters or Victims?" *CourtTV Crime Library.*
4. Russell, Diana E.H., *Against Pornography: The Evidence of Harm*, Russell Publications, 1994.
5. Hughes, Donna Rice, "Recent Statistics on Internet Dangers," *ProtectKids.com.*
6. "Porn Addiction." The National Campaign to Stop Pornography.
7. "Ohio Group Wants Law to Keep Porn Out of Sex Offenders' Hands." Focus on the Family, *Citizenlink.com*, Sept. 21, 2006.

Chapter Seventeen: The Thieves

1. "Kidnapped Missouri Baby Found Alive." *CBS News*, Sept. 20, 2006.
2. "Maine Parents Charged With Kidnapping Pregnant Daughter." *FoxNews.com*, Sept. 18, 2006.

Chapter Eighteen: The Unbelievers

1. London, H.B. Jr., "Alarmed By The Alarm." *The Pastor's Weekly Briefing*, Focus on the Family Pastoral Ministries.

Chapter Nineteen: The Unforgiving

1. Young, Thomas H., "Director's Report," *HBR Report*, National Association of Letter Carriers, Jan. 2005.

978-0-595-45424-2
0-595-45424-0